AF731873

Transportation Sector in India and EU

Published in association with
Observer Research Foundation
New Delhi

Observer Research Foundation (ORF) is a public policy think-tank that aims to influence formulation of policies for building a strong and prosperous India. The ORF pursues these goals by providing informed and productive inputs, in-depth research and stimulating discussion. The Foundation is supported in its mission by a cross-section of India's leading public figures, academics and business leaders.

Supported by
Rosa Luxemburg Stiftung
New Delhi

The Rosa Luxemburg Stiftung (RLS) is one of the largest political education institutions in Germany today and sees itself as part of the intellectual current of democratic socialism. The foundation evolved from a small political group, "Social Analysis and Political Education Association", founded in 1990 in Berlin into a nationwide political education organisation, a discussion forum for critical thought and political alternatives, as well as a research facility for progressive social analysis.

Transportation Sector in India and EU

Problems, Prospects and Opportunities for Development

Editor

Rumi Aijaz

ACADEMIC FOUNDATION
NEW DELHI

www.academicfoundation.com

First published in 2014
by

ACADEMIC FOUNDATION
4772-73 / 23 Bharat Ram Road, (23 Ansari Road),
Darya Ganj, New Delhi - 110 002 (India).
Phones : 23245001 / 02 / 03 / 04.
Fax : +91-11-23245005.
E-mail : books@academicfoundation.com
www.academicfoundation.com

in association with the
Observer Research Foundation, New Delhi

Supported by:
Rosa Luxemburg Stiftung, New Delhi

Disclaimer:
The opinions/views/findings expressed in this book are solely those of the authors and do not necessarily reflect the views of the publisher.

© 2014
Copyright: Observer Research Foundation, New Delhi

ALL RIGHTS RESERVED.
No part of this book shall be reproduced, stored in a retrieval system, or transmitted by any means, electronic, mechanical, photocopying, recording, or otherwise, without the prior written permission of the copyright holder(s) and/or the publishers.

Cataloging in Publication Data--DK
Courtesy: D.K. Agencies (P) Ltd. <docinfo@dkagencies.com>

Transportation sector in India and EU : problems, prospects and opportunities for development / editor, Rumi Aijaz.
pages cm
Includes bibliographical references (pages).
ISBN 9789332701526

1. Transportation--India--Congresses. 2. Transportation and state--India--Congresses. 3. Transportation--Environmental aspects--India--Congresses. 4. European Union--India--Congresses. I. Aijaz, Rumi, editor. II. Observer Research Foundation.

DDC 388.0954 23

Typeset by Italics India, New Delhi.

Printed and bound by The Book Mint, New Delhi.
www.thebookmint.in

Contents

List of Tables, Figures and Boxes

Tables

Figures

Boxes

About the Workshop Organisers

The Observer Research Foundation (ORF) is India's premier think tank engaged in developing and discussing policy alternatives on a wide-range of issues of national and international significance. The fundamental objective of ORF is to aid and influence formulation of policies for building a strong and prosperous India. ORF pursues its goal of providing productive inputs to decision-makers in the government, civil society and the business leadership of India through in-depth research and stimulating discussions. ORF firmly believes that in the next 25 years, India will be one of the world's greatest economic powers and contribute to a significant transformation in the quality of life of humanity.

The Foundation was established in the early nineties during the troubled period of India's transition from a protected economy to a new engagement with the international economic order. At that time, a need was felt for an independent forum that would examine the critical problems facing the country and help develop coherent policy responses in a rapidly changing global environment. ORF was thus founded and subsequently supported by many of India's leading intellectuals, academics, public figures, social activists, business leaders and institutions of higher learning. Headquartered in New Delhi, ORF has chapters in Chennai, Kolkata and Mumbai. The key areas of research undertaken by ORF include: international relations, security, resources management, politics, governance, economy and development.

ORF views collaboration with think tanks and research organisations across the globe as a vital part of its mandate. For international partners, ORF represents an institution that is able to generate real-time and quality analysis on a diverse range of public policy issues. ORF believes that collaborative exercises must be initiated and sustained as equal partnerships in conceptualisation, funding and management. Some important partners are Rosa Luxemburg Stiftung, Germany; ZEIT Stiftung Ebelin und Gerd Bucerius, Germany; Heritage Foundation, USA; Brookings Institution, USA; Fudan University, China. More information about ORF is available at *www.orfonline.org*.

The Rosa Luxemburg Stiftung (RLS) is one of the largest political education institutions in Germany today and sees itself as part of the intellectual current of democratic socialism. The foundation evolved from a small political group, "Social Analysis and Political Education Association", founded in 1990 in Berlin, into a nationwide political education organisation, a discussion forum for critical thought and political alternatives, as well as a research facility for progressive social analysis. In 1996, RLS was officially recognised as a nationwide affiliated trust of the Party of Democratic Socialism (PDS), presently known as "DIE LINKE" (The Left). As such, it works closely with DIE LINKE-affiliated state foundations and associations nationwide.

RLS aims to: organise political education and disseminate knowledge about social relations in a globalised, unjust and hostile world; provide a venue for critical analysis of current capitalism; act as a hub for programmatic discussions about a modern democratic socialism; act as a socialistic think tank for political alternatives; be a forum in Germany and internationally that supports dialogue between left-socialistic powers, socialistic movements and organisations, left-minded intellectuals and non-governmental organisations; grant funding to young scholars *via* undergraduate and postgraduate scholarships; give impulses to self-defining socialistic political activities and support commitment to peace and international understanding for a socially just and solitary union.

Forming the RLS are: the general and sustaining members of the association and the executive board members; academic scholars and scientists in advisory boards and as authors of RLS publications, scholarship recipients, liaison professors and hundreds of volunteers; more than 100 employees that work in the Academy for Political

Education, the Centre for International Dialogue and Cooperation, the Institute for Critical Social Analysis, etc. More information about RLS is available at *www.rosalux.de/english/foundation.html.*

About the Editor/Contributors

Editor:

Rumi Aijaz is Senior Fellow at the Observer Research Foundation (ORF), New Delhi. His educational qualifications include a Master's in Geography (Jawaharlal Nehru University, 1992) and Regional Planning (School of Planning and Architecture, 1994), and PhD in Urban Governance (School of Planning and Architecture, 2004). He has been a post-doctoral visiting fellow at the Asia Research Centre, London School of Economics and Political Science (2006). He is also an associate member of the Institute of Town Planners, India.

He has worked with the non-government organisation 'Sanket' (1994-95), and the National Institute of Urban Affairs (1996-1999 and 2004-05). He has also undertaken a study on gender for the Royal Netherlands Embassy (1996-97). During his education and professional career, he has been involved in numerous studies covering a range of social science topics such as urbanisation, transportation, socioeconomic and human development, ecology and physical environment, women empowerment and public health.

His writings and views on different urban topics have found place in leading world journals, including *Habitat International* (Elsevier) and *Journal of Asian and African Studies* (Sage), and acknowledged by prominent Indian and foreign institutions and news agencies. His book titled *Democracy and Urban Governance in India* (Academic Foundation, 2012) describes innovative urban policy measures and governance practices designed and introduced by the Indian government at local government level to address contemporary urban challenges. Another edited volume titled *Global Urbanisation Experiences* (Academic Foundation, 2013), comprises 10 papers contributed by experts from Asia, Europe, Latin America and USA on important urban topics such as city planning and design, transport system, world city network, energy management and social exclusion.

Contributors:

Kaushik Ranjan Bandyopadhyay is Associate Professor in the Department of Business Sustainability at TERI University. He is an applied economist with 15 years of research and teaching experience. During this period, he has worked on a range of areas, including energy, climate change, transport, human development, poverty, human rights, public finance and regional cooperation. His current research interests include sustainable business strategy, sustainability reporting, sustainable and disruptive innovation, corporate social responsibility, renewable energy policy, shale gas policy, oil and gas pricing, energy subsidies, transport policy, climate change and energy security.

Rohit Chaturvedi is Director (Transport, Logistics and Infra Finance), CRISIL Risk and Infrastructure Solutions Limited, based in Mumbai. Previously, he has been Director (Projects), Principal Consultant (Senior Manager) and Project Delivery Head at i-maritime Consultancy Private Limited. He has been educated at Indian Institute of Management, Bangalore and Kumaun University.

Anjali Goyal is an officer from the Indian Railway Services (1985 Civil Services Exam), presently working on deputation to Planning Commission, Ministry of Planning as Adviser, Project Appraisal and Management Division. In her previous assignment as Executive Director (Finance) in the Ministry of Railways she handled the railway budget for three years and has worked extensively on dedicated freight corridor, high-speed rail corridors and public private participation initiatives of the Ministry of Railways. She has published papers on the subject of low-carbon structuring of dedicated freight corridor and high-speed rail projects and strategy for bringing high speed rail to India.

Anshul Gupta is Executive Director, Corporate Coordination at RailTel Corporation of India Limited. He has received his education from Indian Institute of Science (Bangalore), George Mason University (Virginia), and Management Development Institute (Gurgaon). He specialises in design and development of modern signalling and safety systems, conceptualisation of software embedded train borne control systems, quality system assurance for signalling and telecom products.

Bernhard Knierim is a biophysicist and political scientist, and is working with the NGO "Bahn für Alle" ("Railways for everyone") that helped to prevent the privatisation of the German railways. He is also currently working as a scientific assistant for Sabine Leidig, member of the German parliament, and regularly writes for different journals. He has recently completed a master's in public policy.

Hermann Knoflacher has been a professor at the Vienna University of Technology in Austria since 1975. In 1985, he became Head of the Institute for Transport Planning. His research focuses on spatial planning, urban planning and transport planning. He is one of the key contributors to the sustainable transport movement. He is well known for his criticism of excessive automobile usage and its effects on humans and the environment. Since 2004, he is the president of the Club of Vienna. He is also a member of the Club of Budapest and the global pedestrian representative of the United Nations.

Pawan Kumar is Associate Town and Country Planner with the Town and Country Planning Organisation, New Delhi. His educational qualifications include Bachelor of Architecture, Master of Planning and PhD in Transportation.

Anuradha Shukla is Chief Scientist and Advisor (R&D) at Central Road Research Institute (CRRI), New Delhi. She joined CRRI in 1986 as a scientist. Until December 2011, she has been divisional head responsible for transportation planning and environment. Her specific expertise is in national and international environmental pollution due to roads and transportation. She has published more than 80 papers in journals and conferences. She is also the Fulbright Fellow for Environmental Leadership Programme. Her educational qualifications include a PhD (Jamia Millia Islamia, Delhi), MSc (IIT, Delhi), MTech (IIT, Bombay) and Post Graduate Diploma in Ecology and Environment. Her PhD thesis is on Real World On-Road Emissions of In-Use Vehicles.

1

RUMI AIJAZ

Editorial Introduction

The manner in which the transport sector has been developed and is being maintained in some countries is widely criticised. Negative opinions are often formed about the government's capability in handling the sector due to the persistent presence of numerous mobility-related problems and the weak response to challenges and needs.

For a government, it is necessary to change this mind set by ensuring that all citizens have greater access to their needs and that various (economic) activities operate and flourish at desirable levels. This fundamental goal can be achieved to a great extent by providing an efficient transport network system.

The implications of not providing adequate transport facilities and services can be enormous for a nation, as shown below:

- Countries will fare poorly in development indices.
- Governments will be at risk of losing credibility and power.
- Many sectors of the economy and development will suffer thereby leading to the possibility of occurrence of insurgency.
- Social and economic inequalities will show a sharp rise.
- People will face difficulties, spend more and loose time in acquiring basic needs such as health and education.
- Environment and health impacts of traffic emissions will be immense.
- Problem of insecurity during mobility will grow among all citizens, including pedestrians, children, women and men.
- Migration to urban areas will grow due to lack of regional transport services.

Huge challenges in the transportation sector are observed in current times. For example, in developing countries such as India, linkages between rural and urban settlements are weak, pedestrian needs are ignored and share of public transport vehicles is low. This has led to a phenomenal growth of private motor vehicles that emit harmful gases. Further, due to use of outdated technologies and incomplete planning, there are major problems of traffic congestion, women's safety and accidents.

Traffic and transportation-related problems of various types are also visible in many developed countries, where much work is being done for: promotion of non-motorised vehicles due to the growing vehicular congestion; mitigation of noise; reduction of vehicular emissions; ensuring road safety; mobilisation of revenue for implementing new projects; and transportation of goods efficiently within urban areas.

Thus, in some countries of the world, governments realise that the goals of high economic growth, balanced development and poverty alleviation can be achieved by developing the transportation sector in ways that provide for enhanced and safe mobility of persons. In the context of developing nations, it is further understood that: providing reliable and sufficient public transport services to relocated slum dwellers can pull them out of extreme poverty; improving sanitary and environmental conditions in bus stands and railway stations could be a useful step in attracting commuters from various income classes to public transport services; using technology to set up integrated passenger information systems, common ticketing systems, etc., will work as a boon for commuters; using technology in tendering process and in awarding contracts would address the issue of corruption in projects; using indicators to measure quality of transport governance would go a long way in overall improvement of the sector; and establishing partnerships can help in delivering improved transport and accessibility.

Many Western and European scholars argue that the mistakes committed by their governments in the name of development must not be repeated in developing parts of the world, and that any kind of policy making and planning must take into account human behaviour, their movements and requirements, and the ways in which settlements evolve.

ORF-RLS Workshops on Transportation

Observer Research Foundation (ORF) with the support of the Rosa Luxemburg Stiftung (RLS) organised two workshops on transportation, one in Berlin and the other in Delhi during 2011-12 to discuss and invite expert opinions on the key problems confronting the transport sector and the improvement strategies needed. The workshops were organised under the European-Asian Policy Dialogue pursued by the two institutions.

About the Publication

This edited volume presents a collection of eight papers which provide information on the transportation sector in India and EU. The compilation is an outcome of the papers presented during the two ORF-RLS workshops. It is intended to help readers having interest in the field of transport in building a superior understanding of the problems, prospects and opportunities for development in the transportation sector. The papers have been contributed by leading subject experts both from India and EU, who are affiliated with renowned institutions and have been making numerous efforts for the improvement of the sector.

The papers describe various local, regional and national dimensions of the transport sector including:

- pedestrian and eco-friendly systems of travel,
- private sector participation in railways,
- railways' share in transport market and the economic impact of railways,
- rail signalling and telecommunication systems,
- road traffic and air pollution scenario,
- inland waterways,
- energy consumption and CO_2 emissions from road transport.

The contributing authors have explained how improvements can be achieved in rail, road and waterways sector, and proposed measures for building enhanced mobility systems which are environment friendly and sustainable.

Also provided at the end of this volume is a bibliography of publications on transport.

Paper Abstracts

The society was and remains fascinated by motorised transport that other aspects of the transport sector have been completely overlooked. Hermann Knoflacher submits that while the physical environment has been changed with the implementation of transport policies, it has been done without thinking how people will adapt to it. Attention is drawn to advantages of using pedestrian and eco-friendly systems of travel, and the measures needed to achieve this goal.

The government usually claims not having enough financial resources for the development of railways, so the involvement of private investors is generally regarded as one option. By analysing different railway privatisation models functioning in Europe, Bernhard Knierim concludes that privatisation does not always lead to favourable results and therefore, a modern and affordable railway system should be built by generating revenue from other less environmentally friendly modes of transport.

Can Indian railways claim pride of place as a sustainable transport in India? Based on various reality checks in the areas of railways' share in transport market and the economic impact of railways, Anjali Goyal observes that the goal of sustainability is far from achieved. It is suggested that a sustainable railway will have to significantly increase its market share to be economically and socially viable, which requires triggering a decisive modal shift from road to rail. Some strategies to make railways a sustainable transport are put forward by the author.

With constraints in line capacity and cases of safety breach due to staff failure, Indian railways is looking for substantial improvement in their signalling and safety systems through adoption of modern technologies at optimal cost. Anshul Gupta identifies the gaps in the present system and suggests technology which can not only support legacy systems but is also able to integrate with new signalling and telecommunication systems of Indian railways.

Transportation emissions are a major cause of air pollution in Indian cities that adversely affect the health of the people and their quality of life. Anuradha Shukla examines the road traffic and air pollution scenario in Delhi, and observes that a lack of integrated land-use and transport planning has led to extreme congestion, ever slowing speeds, increase in road accidents, fuel wastage and environmental pollution. She suggests that there is a need to focus on appropriate travel demand management measures to relieve road congestion and pollution.

Every day a significant amount of travel is done on foot. However, pedestrian needs are considerably lacking. Pawan Kumar expresses concern over the prevailing deficiencies in pedestrian planning, design, infrastructure, and points out that people who travel by foot are at great risk of injury and harassment. Pedestrian planning should be considered as an integral part of overall transport system; to this end, he outlines a series of measures to ensure pedestrian safety.

The concept of inland waterways as an alternative transport system scores over its counterparts in many aspects like less fuel consumption, less dependence on land and protection of water bodies. Rohit Chaturvedi explores the option of inland waterways as an alternative to the existing transport system in Mumbai and as a supplement to the multi-modal transport model. He concludes that enthusiasm to develop inland waterways is sorely lacking due to a number of challenges in the areas of regulation, administration, design and finance.

In view of the fact that the transport sector has been largely responsible for the pollution and greenhouse gas emissions, Kaushik Ranjan Bandyopadhyay in his paper focuses on challenges and opportunities of reducing energy consumption and CO_2 emissions from road transport in India.

2

HERMANN KNOFLACHER

Integrated Transport Policy

How to Make a Non-working Vision a Reality

The Fascination with Mechanical Transport Modes

The era of fossil powered transport systems was dominated by sectoral transport policy separating railways, public transport and road traffic from each other. In many countries, one ministry is responsible for railways and another for roads, but so far no ministry has been given the responsibility for pedestrians or cyclists. The society was and remains fascinated by the opportunities of technical modes—first the railway, then the car and the airplane—that transport policy has lost footing. Institutes and institutions were established to separately handle each of these two technical modes, regardless of what was happening in the other parts of the transport sector. Railways dominated the 19th century and the first half of the 20th century; cars became the dominant mode in the second half of the 20th century. The share of public transport in Germany was reduced from 65 per cent of all mechanical trips in 1950 to 17 per cent in the year 2000.

Transport Policy in the Second Half of the 20th Century

European transport policy followed for decades the transport policy of the winner of the Second World War, the United States, before the society and experts realised the terrible damage being done to European urban structure and infrastructure by following the American car-oriented transport ideology. The first energy crisis in 1973 did not change the transport policy very much, since each sector of mechanical mobility tried to find its own solution for the problem. There was no wide awareness of the reality of the system. At the end of the 20th century, the society became aware of climate change and the limited fossil fuel resources, mentioned already in the report to the Club of Rome 1972. The keyword 'sustainability' was applied to every human activity, including the transport sector. Multimodality has gone hand in hand with the slogan of sustainability in the transport sector since about 20 years.

Difference between Vision and Policy

Each policy has a certain vision or goal, usually encompassed in a slogan. Policies are real measures intervening in the system to reach a certain goal. Multimodal transport policy has therefore no meaning as long as there are no goals casted in figures, fixed in time and budget. To make a vision a reality different from the existing one, measures have to be implemented effectively to change the behaviour of the system in such a way that it moves toward the goals of the vision.

Transport policy over the last 200 years has proven that it can successfully lead to transport problems, environment degradation, social separation, urban sprawl and increasing financial deficits. Since the modern transport system is manmade, creating all these unwanted, unexpected adverse effects, people dealing with the system have unsurprisingly not understood the reality of the transport system behaviour. There are several obvious causes, and one of them is the lack of scientific background to transport practices implemented thus far. What is called 'Transport Science' are guilds, separated into technicians, economists, lawyers and politicians, each of them collected around assumptions and short-time experience without a common understanding of the transport system behaviour.

Existing Integrated Transport Policy: Not More than a Slogan

There are commendable goals for an integrated transport policy that combine 'political integration,' 'technical integration' and 'social integration,' no matter the nuances these terms may themselves comprise. This should ideally lead toward a sustainable future-oriented development in the transport sector. But the real effects of this kind of transport policy are not encouraging at all. The outcome of the real activities on the state level are not more than slogans and symptom-oriented measures, where states try to combine railway with road administration and add some cyclists and pedestrians into the mix. In the western context, integrated transport policy means the integration of mechanical transport modes without understanding the real transport system behaviour. But the basic approach does not change. If transport disciplines were scientific, it would be possible to say that 'integrated transport policy is built on a wrong paradigm.' Since a paradigm is based on core hypotheses, the hypotheses being used to build the policy are probably wrong. The existing integrated transport policy is therefore following misleading indicators.

Basic Pillars of Existing Transport Policy and the Reality of the Transport System Behaviour

Technical transport modes were developed in the last 200 years without understanding their effects on the real world. Within a few decades, many people had more or less direct access to a transport system providing them with a speed they have never experienced before in the history of mankind. At the same time, technical transport modes were able to transport goods over long distances in short time, again as had never occurred before. The recognisable immediate effects were so convincing and encouraging that no one thought of the flipside. None of the existing disciplines in universities have therefore understood the real system behaviour. They formed pillars based on assumptions of personal experiences in the transport system and misused terms not fully understood. For example, mobility, as understood in the current concept of a transport system, is everything which moves with technical means and is not related to purposes: it is a purposeless mobility. Transport means movements of vehicles on or in special transport channels not taking into account the origin and the destination. The system view was a cross-section view of road or rail in the traffic engineering field. Three assumptions are at the base of existing transport policy:

- Growth of mobility.
- Time saving by increasing speed.
- Freedom of modal choice.

In contradiction to these assumptions, the transport system behaviour is completely different.

- There is no growth of mobility if mobility is defined with purpose in mind. If the number of people in a society does not change, the number of trips per people per day remains the same. This has been proven over the course of several decades. There is only a shift in the mode of transport, but there is no change in the number of trips. A definition of mobility must be related to purpose. In a qualified scientific world, there are no longer any doubts about these facts.
- In the transport system, increasing transport speed does not equal saving time. Each trip is connected with the origin and destination. If the speed is increasing, the location of origin and/or the location of destination is changing. This means speed changes the physical structures without changing the travel time. Travel time constancy has been proven in all observations over the decades; however, this has not been accepted by economists, who are still calculating benefits from a figure which does not exist. It has further not been accepted by engineers, who believe in what they individually experience or believe to have experienced, because they have not understood the difference between the combination of man and machine on the one hand and man as the source of most of the politicians and society on the other.
- There is no freedom of choice for real people. It is obvious that there is no freedom of choice for people without means to choose expensive transport modes. But it is not so obvious that the structure is determining human behaviour in such a way that commuters do not have a total free choice either, given physical structures are influencing their behaviour. To understand transport system behaviour, it is therefore necessary to understand human behaviour in general and in the artificial modified environment of today in particular.

Existing Multimodal Transport Policy is Treating Symptoms and Not Causes

Multimodal transport policy is dealing with symptoms, if it is dealing with transport flows. Transport flows are visible symptoms of causes in the background—often not easy to discover or recognise. If the causes are in the field of other disciplines, they are not visible from the narrow world view of specialists. Since the prevailing measures of multimodal transport policy are not successful as expected, attempts are made to make more of them. But a mistake cannot be solved by aggravating it. Clearly, the existing structures do not produce the expected and wanted behaviour of the system and its users.

This shows that integrated transport policy has to treat structures and not symptoms of the transport system if it should be successful. This is the basic lack in the existing integrated transport policy worldwide: its core elements are transport modes, but transport modes are not the cause, only the mean for certain purposes.

The Core of Any Multimodal Transport Policy

To find the key element for multimodal transport policy, the cause has to be identified, i.e., the man and his behaviour. Human behaviour needs to be understood not only on the psychological level, but in an evolutionary context. Looking at various disciplines will reveal the real cause and not only its effects. Evolutionary epistemology is consequently a necessary tool. The physical environment has changed fundamentally with transport policy but without any consideration to how people will adapt to it. People have adjusted perfectly from their individual point of view—but with all the adverse system effects, nobody wanted to have. To understand this behaviour-change, it was necessary to find the causal level, deeply rooted in our evolutionary history.

Human behaviour is driven by body energy consumption, physical and mental. Body energy consumption per time was a successful selection element during evolution. Using vehicles instead of walking reduces body energy consumption substantially and makes distant destinations easy accessible—the individual benefit. The energy consumption of the technical mode in the system is recognised by our senses. What is not recognised are the other structural changes in the system: nearness is lost everywhere, dependency on fossil energy is mounting, noise and air pollution increases, local job opportunities are lost, international corporations dominate municipalities and even states and societies are separated, etc.

To change human behaviour, the structures have to be first and foremost changed.

The Basic Mistake in the Transport System of Today: Missing Common Entity

Since man and transport system was not understood, the core element for a successful multimodal transport policy is missing. Since it is missing, it is not recognised that a multimodal policy can never be successful with a large number of uncoordinated activities, many of them being, in fact, counterproductive. Take, for example, the EU transport policy to remove bottlenecks in the road and rail network, which does not realise that the feedback effect of the policy is continuously producing newer and bigger bottlenecks elsewhere. Indian transport policy is even faster in the manner in which bigger unintended consequences have sprouted, given the manner in which flyovers and motorways were built in its megacities, destroying precious vital urban structures in a society of pedestrians and cyclists. The core element is not the technical transport mode, as experts and politicians believe, and neither is it the road or rail network or the financial structure (although these have some effect).

The Core Entity of Any Multimodal Transport Policy is Man

The fundamental element is man in his real evolutionary condition. Only if man is at the core of all measures can multimodality be realised in the transport system. It is therefore a must to look for measures which touch the basest of all levels of human behaviour: body energy.

People's body energy is replaced or compensated by technical transport modes driven by artificial energy at points of origin and destination of every trip. If these points are organised in a faulty manner, multimodality is no longer possible. Existing transport science and policy has neither recognised this key element nor the real behaviour of people. They have just provided transport systems of different kinds, but have not considered the interactions between them and everything they are connecting—and separating. And people 'read' these physical structures and behave as they have behaved since man existed: selfishly and intelligently.

The Key for a Multimodal Transport Policy: A Different Parking Regime

The key for all the problems in the transport, environmental, sociological and economic sector is the erroneous organisation of parking. If cars can be parked close to human activities, everybody is trapped in the car and cannot escape due to his evolutionary, physiological structure. Parking close to human activities destroys the quality of life everywhere, damages local business and employment, destroys the chance of choice for public transport, and deteriorates the environment for all generations, particularly for children.

It is very difficult and perhaps even impossible to convince somebody living under these structural, physical conditions to use public transport, cycle or walk. In highly motorised countries, most of the destinations are not accessible for pedestrians and cyclists anymore. To implement a successful transport policy, the key problem has to be treated: parking organisation. This is already happening in some cities. Since transport policies are measures, the key measure for a realistic, successful multimodal transport policy is the spatial separation between human activities and parked vehicles.

There are different principle solutions: to give people the chance of choice between cars and public transport, car parks must be at least as far away as the next public transport stop. This means that people live, work, shop and recreate in car-free areas. Only handicapped people and delivery vehicles can enter these areas.

This is the model which is intuitively implemented in many cities today. This is also the model where success has been achieved through pedestrianising historical city centres. To pedestrianise a historical city centre is not very difficult: as soon as cars are removed from the city centre, it starts to thrive. Shops come back, business increases.

It is a tragedy that India has not recognised the opportunity to overcome all the problems the Europeans had by copying the American transport policy. If the walled city in Delhi, like all the other historical urban structures in Indian cities, were to become car- and motorcycle-free, it would be the most attractive living place if combined with public transport. Moreover, instead of seizing the opportunity that India's long cycling tradition (something any European state would be proud of) has to offer, the administration is following the advice of old-fashioned experts who have no idea about the real needs of human life and no effective responsibility. The area of Chandini Chowk has been run aground with small, green buses that are destroying the capacity and lifeblood of this famous and wonderful historical city by pushing away pedestrians, cycle rickshaws and cyclists.

Mechanical modes bring noise, accidents and air pollution into liveable human structures. In combination with the metro system in the city, a future-oriented government would pedestrianise the entire Chandni Chowk area.

Examples of Successful Multimodal Policy Measures

Previously in Vienna, the city centre used to be occupied with more than 60,000 cars every day. The effect was a dying urban centre with declining businesses. In 1968, the city government was convinced to pedestrianise the urban centre. Plans were implemented in 1974 in conjunction with the opening of the underground. Today, this part of the city has become the most vibrant, economic and successful area not only of the city but also of the country. The turnover of shops has increased even though no car traffic is allowed outside the delivery period between 7 and 10 o'clock in the morning. The same is happening in all the other parts of the world where cars are being removed from public space as well as from private local garages. Another example is the quarter of Vauban, Freiburg, where 4,500 residents live in a car-free area. Sixty-seven per cent of the residents gave up their car-ownership when settling in Vauban.

Since the urban master plan of 1981 has been implemented in the city of Vienna step by step, with changes in the city's structure by pushing out parked cars from roads as well as from private yards and garages, the situation has changed dramatically over the last decades. Since 2002, the degree of motorisation in Vienna has decreased, despite the fact that the Viennese are the richest people in Austria. The structure has changed and people have recognised that they can live much better and much easier without cars. There is no free parking place within the inner districts anymore, not even on private ground. Since the number of people has increased and the number of trips is constant, there is greater mobility in the system, but not in cars. The share of public transport is increasing, as well as the number of cyclists and pedestrians. This is a typical example of an integrated transport policy taking into account the causes and not the symptoms. Integrated transport policy can only be successful if parking regulations are changed fundamentally, as per the recommendations of the instruction leaflet of the Austrian Society for Transport Science.

The Big Chance for Countries with Low Degree of Motorisation: Learn from European Mistakes

The knowledge of today shows that India as well as all the other countries which are not trapped in car dependency like the western high-motorised other states have the opportunity to leapfrog the terrible mistakes of the last five decades in the transport policy of the western society and reach a sustainable transport system future earlier than the high-motorised countries. This can only happen if India is able to change the education and administration system which is still thinking and working in the mainstream, thus leading to transport problems and not solutions.

3

BERNHARD KNIERIM

Private Sector Participation in Railways?

Railways as the Most Environmentally Friendly and Efficient Mode of Transportation

There is no doubt any more that the increasing emissions of carbon dioxide (CO_2) due to the burning of fossil energy reserves lead to global warming [Intergovernmental Panel on Climate Change (IPCC), 2007]. While an average world citizen should only emit up to 2.7 tonnes (t) of CO_2 per year if the global rise of the temperature level is to be kept at least below 2°C with a high probability, the average was already 4.5 t of CO_2 per world citizen in 2010. The average Indian citizen, however, only emits 1.2 t of CO_2 (this is an average—the Indian middle class is also well above the limit already), while the average German emits 10 t of CO_2 and the average US-American even 19.5 t (Figure 3.1). This illustrates a huge global imbalance: while the countries that have already been industrialised for a longer time have mainly caused the climate change problem, the whole world is suffering from it together. Some countries emitting comparably little CO_2 per person like Bangladesh are the most affected by climate change.

About one-fifth of the CO_2 emissions are caused by transport, making it the second biggest source (Figure 3.2). While anything reducing the need for transportation is certainly the best way to reduce energy usage and therewith CO_2 emissions, the mode of transport also makes a vast difference. A typical trip in Germany from Berlin to Frankfurt illustrates this: driving a car alone would require 41.7 litres of gasoline, a flight would be slightly better with 37.8 litres (converted), but a train ride would only take 11.2 litres—and is thus about four times better.

Figure 3.1

Global CO_2 Emissions

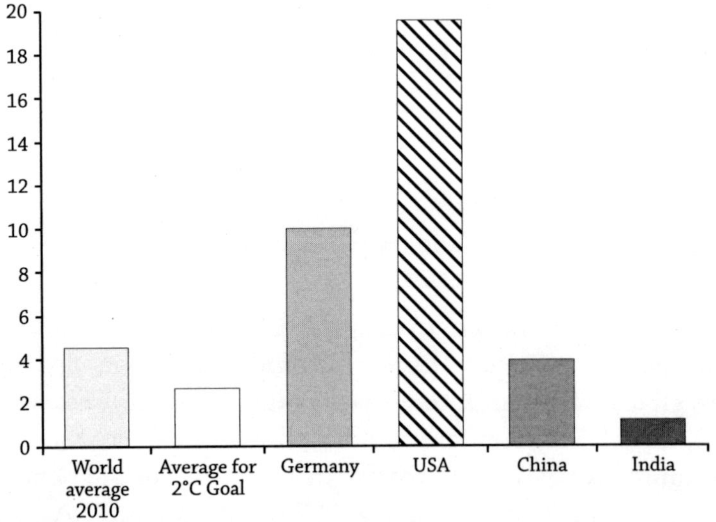

Source: The World Bank Data.

Figure 3.2

Sources of CO_2 Emissions, Europe

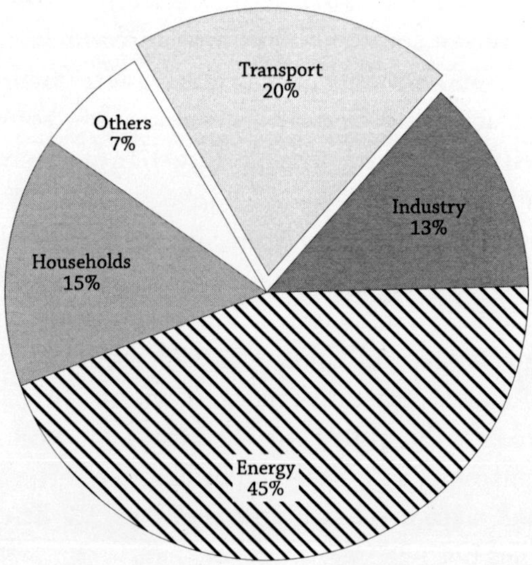

Source: European Commission.

This is also mirrored in railway CO_2 emissions, which are less than a quarter of those of a car, and emissions of particulate matter, which are only about 10 per cent compared to a car's (Figure 3.3) (IFEU, 2011). The total time needed for the three different modes of transport is about the same, if the trips to and from the airport or station, security check, etc., are taken into account: around 4.5 hours. But a look at the prices shows where politics come into play: the train trip is the most expensive (89 € = ₹ 5,785), while the flight (63 € = ₹ 4,095) and driving the car (58 € = ₹ 3,754—only for gasoline-driven cars) are cheaper. This shows how the economic incentives are not beneficial for the environment. Prices are highly political, because they are strongly affected by both subsidies and taxes (e.g., kerosene for airplanes is tax-free, while the railway trip is under the full energy tax). Interestingly, this is not the case for India, where a train ticket between Delhi and Tamil Nadu is only about 10 per cent of the price of the cheapest air fare—but the train trip also takes 40 hours as opposed to 5-hour flight.

Generally, the emission data shows that per person-kilometre, railways only emit a third of the CO_2 as opposed to cars and an eighth as opposed to an airplane, similar fractions of nitric oxides (NO_x) and even lower amounts of particulate matter. The same advantages are true for freight transport, with even better results for the railways as compared to the other modes.

There is a very simple physical reason why railways are much more energy efficient than any road transportation: the rolling resistance between a train wheel and the steel rail is only about 0.2 per cent of the weight, while the rolling resistance between a rubber tire and the road is 10 times more: 2 per cent of the weight. This means if one wants to move a 40 t lorry on a road, this requires the same force as lifting 800 kg; if one wants to move a 40 t rail car on a steel rail, a force equivalent to lifting 80 kg is sufficient. In addition, trains are also better in terms of wind resistance, because the rail cars are very close to each other, while each car or lorry has its own wind resistance. As for any kind of air transport, it is of course even more energy intensive because the complete weight has to be lifted up into the air. The energy to lift the whole airplane up to about 10 km above

Figure 3.3

Energy Usage and Emissions for the Trip from Berlin to Frankfurt

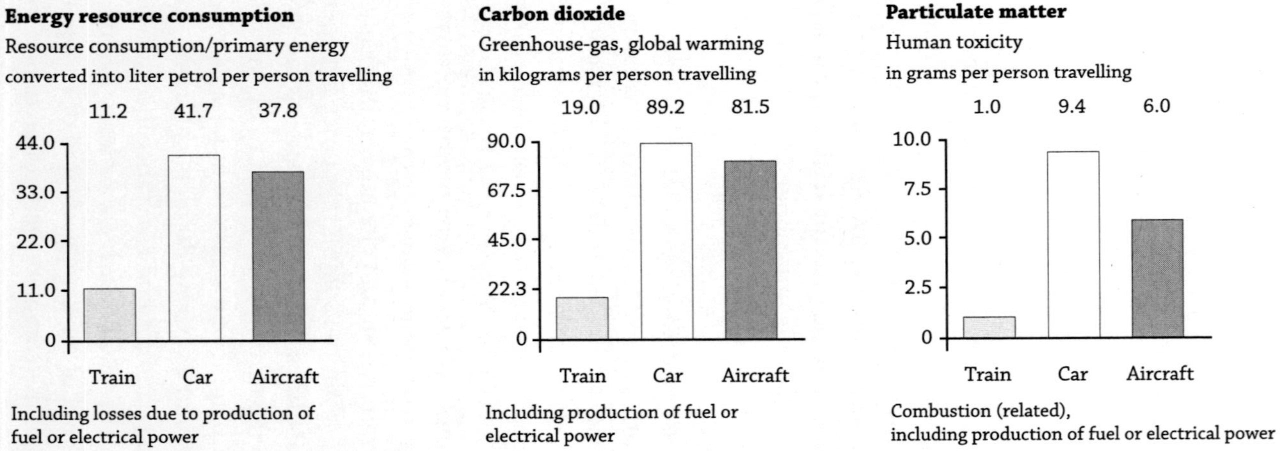

Source: IFEU Institute. Transport Emission Model.

the surface of the earth is particularly significant in short-distance flights. Moreover, railways, if electrified, can be used with different sources of energy, especially renewable sources, and as opposed to electric cars, they do not need to carry the weight of the energy storage.

All transportation causes external costs—not only due to climate damage (14%), environmental damage (10%) and to pollution and noise (12%), but also due to accidents (52%). These external costs are never included in the price of the transportation itself, so they are not borne by the producers but by the community. The external costs of road transportation in Germany alone is estimated to be at least € 60 billion (₹ 3,900 billion) (Kolodziej *et al.*, 2009), though some estimate it to be twice as high. If these numbers were included in the expenses for transportation, the cost relationship would be completely different, making railways cheaper in relation to road and air traffic. In the system today, which also includes heavy subsidies for all modes of transport, there is simply no truth in traffic costs. Unfortunately, this leads to greater attraction towards more harmful modes of transport.

In addition to the energy usage and the emissions, railways and public transit in general are also preferable due to social reasons. As opposed to a car, public transit does not require any investment upfront by the user and is, therefore, also affordable for less affluent people and can be used by those who simply do not want to own a car. Furthermore, trains can also be used by disabled and elderly people on their own as well by children.

How to Make Railways More Attractive

At present, railways have a rather small share of the transportation market in most countries. For example, in Germany, only 7.6 per cent of the passenger traffic and 17.3 per cent of the freight traffic are by rail, while 79.5 per cent and 70.6 per cent of passenger and freight traffic respectively are road bound (Figure 3.4).

In India, the situation is better for the railways with a market share of 13.3 per cent in passenger traffic and 39.9 per cent in freight

Figure 3.4

Modal Split in Germany

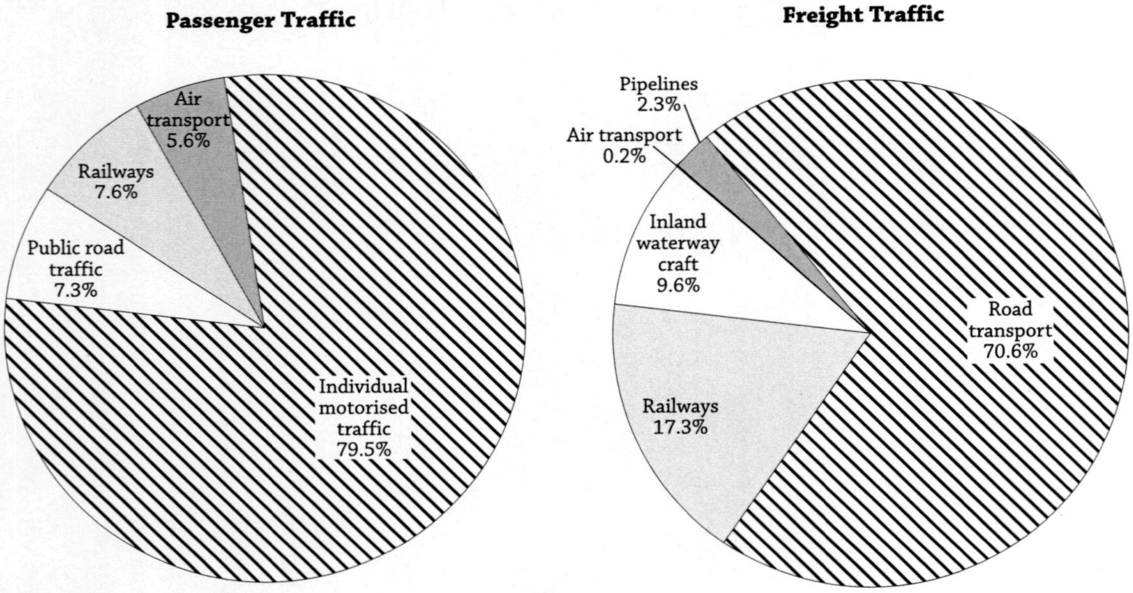

Source: Verkehr in Zahlen (Bundesministerium für Verkehr, Bau und Stadtentwicklung).

transport, but those shares have also decreased over the last 40 years (Table 3.1).

Table 3.1

Modal Split in India

Year	*Freight Rail (%)*	*Freight Road (%)*	*Total Freight Traffic (billion tonne-km)*	*Passenger Rail (%)*	*Passenger Road (%)*	*Total Passenger Traffic (billion passenger-km)*
1970-71	65.5	34.5	194.4	32.9	67.1	359.1
1973-74	61.5	38.5	199.1	31.6	68.4	427.6
1976-77	62.3	37.7	251.5	29.7	70.3	549.3
1979-80	54.6	45.4	285.8	27.9	72.1	710.4
1982-83	48.6	51.4	365.9	23.7	76.3	955.9
1985-86	48.7	51.3	422.7	22.2	77.8	1079.2
1988-89	48.0	52.0	505.0	23.0	77.0	1169.0
1999-2000	39.5	60.5	772.2	19.0	81.0	2262.3
2000-01	38.4	61.6	814.4	18.0	82.0	2532.5
2001-02	39.5	60.5	844.2	16.6	83.4	2963.8
2002-03	39.6	60.4	942.2	15.6	84.4	3299.5
2003-04	38.9	61.1	981.2	14.7	85.3	3676.6
2004-05	39.9	60.1	1020.4	13.3	86.7	3881.6

Source: Ministry of Railways; Tata Energy Research Institute.

Thus the question arises: What can be done to make railways more attractive both for passenger traffic and for freight transport?

A Rail Network that Reaches Everywhere

First of all, the whole country should be connected to a rail network. Unfortunately, Germany has been doing the opposite over the last 50 years, and roughly half of the rail network has been shut down. Between 1994 (when the 'railway reform' took place) and 2010 alone, another 16.5 per cent of the network was lost (Table 3.2). Even worse, almost half of the shunting switches and crossings were taken out in an attempt to cut costs. This significantly reduces the capacity and reliability of the rail network, because it takes away opportunities for faster passenger trains to overhaul slower freight trains.

Table 3.2

Rail Network in Germany

Description	*1994*	*2010*	*% Change*
Length of rail network	40,385	33,723	-16.5
Running tracks	78,073	64,077	-17.9
Electrified network	18,934	19,808	+4.6
Shunting switches and crossings	131,968	66,875	-49.0
Private railway sidings	11,742	3,723	-68.5

Source: Verkehr in Zahlen (Bundesministerium für Verkehr, Bau und Stadtentwicklung).

Shutting down railway tracks in rural regions is often justified with those tracks operating at a loss. Generally, train services in rural regions often do not make any profit—but the same is true for other means of transportation such as roads. If the logic that every single connection has to lead to a profit is used everywhere, at first smaller connections are cut. As a consequence other connections are not used as much any longer, because the people living or working along the abandoned connections now use other means of transportation (mostly cars), and therefore the ridership on the larger connections decreases. This leads to a vicious circle where almost all railroad tracks except for a few heavily used connections between large centres are shut down. The same profit logic is rarely used for roads, although roads generally do not generate a profit in rural regions either. It has to be kept in mind that all transportation is always subsidised—especially if the external costs are accounted for. Therefore, subsidies are not generally 'evil,' particularly if they are spent on more environmentally friendly modes of transportation.

If good connections were offered in rural regions, people would increasingly prefer using trains: railways in those regions could become more profitable. There are some examples in Germany where rural railway providers started offering an attractive service with frequent connections and new trains, thereby increasing the ridership 10 times and more.

In India, the rail network is much more wide-meshed than in Germany, but at least it slightly increases instead of a decrease as in Germany. However, if railways are to be an option for transportation in the whole country, the network will have to be expanded further. The aging technique must also be modernised and the fairly low speed of trains therewith increased. A programme to harmonise the different gauges is already underway.

Interconnections with Other Modes of Transportation

Railway service cannot be provided everywhere. In cities, there are generally different options for public transit, and in rural areas, especially in mountainous regions, it does not always make sense to build train tracks. Instead, buses are sometimes a better option. Therefore, it is important to provide good interconnections between railways as the backbone of public transit with other modes of transportation. They can all be teamed in an integrated synchronised timetable which minimises the time to switch between different trains or buses. Enabling one-ticket use would also make usage of all modes of public transport much more attractive.

The combination of bicycles with public transit is another very environmentally friendly option and should be encouraged. This means providing bicycle parking at stations as well as the possibility to take them onto trains.

Integrated Synchronised Timetable

An integrated synchronised timetable (IST) connects trains in different directions in certain so-called 'knots.' There are 'full hour knots' where trains meet at the full hour and 'half hour knots' in which trains meet at mid-hour intervals. All trains arrive at the station shortly before that time and leave it shortly after, and other modes of transit such as tramways or buses can also be included. This enables an optimal timing system without having to wait, thereby making a train system considerably faster without a huge investment for extremely high speeds. The timed transfers also make using the train system much more comfortable; indeed, people almost do not need a timetable any longer, because trains arrive and leave at the same time every hour.

The implementation of such a system requires a large amount of planning and the optimisation of some connections in order to 'fit' between the different knots. Further, it requires stations with enough platforms and the possibility for trains to enter and exit the station at the same time or shortly after each other. A good punctuality of the trains must also be guaranteed, failing which the connections do not work as planned. However, it can be a fairly simple and—compared to high-speed tracks—cheap way to optimise a rail network.

High-speed Rail

High-speed rail is generally praised as a means to modernise a railway system. It is also often seen as a symbol of a country's prestige, with trains like the Shinkansen, the Train à Grande Vitesse (TGV), the InterCity Express (ICE) or the Transrapid exhibiting their national country's industrial power. In India, there are also some high-speed rail corridors under planning.

However, high-speed rail is extremely expensive to build and maintain, and thus only makes sense on longer connections with very high ridership. Energy consumption goes up tremendously with speed, because the resistance on the tracks and wind resistance increase with speed. For a speed of 300 km/hr, there is twice as much energy needed compared to a speed of 200 km/hr—as well as a much higher investment for the tracks and trains. Therefore, a general maximum of speed should be considered. For example, in Germany, some tracks have already been built for 300 km/hr, but now a speed higher than 250 km/hr is seen as uneconomical. Of course, a high-speed connection makes sense in particular if it can then compete with air connections and thus convince people to use railways instead of airplanes. Compared to the energy needed for the flight, railways are generally more economical and more efficient.

Railway Privatisation Models and the Consequences

The presented models to optimise railways are generally very costly. The government usually claims not to have enough financial resources, so the involvement of private investors is generally regarded as another option. There are different methods available to privatise railways, as outlined below.

Selling Everything as an Integrated System

USA has a very wide-meshed railway network today, owned by different freight haulage companies. This model seems to work well for transport of goods (the USA has a comparably higher share of rail transport—almost 40%) on long distances, but for nothing else. The infrastructure is on a low technical standard and only allows very slow speeds, there is almost no electrification, and thus the transport of people is negligible.

The only slightly successful railway privatisation happened in Japan. The Japanese railways were privatised in the 1980s, and now the trains in different regions of the country are operated by different companies. Six of the original nine companies survived and are held together in the 'Japan Railways (JR) Group.' Along with privatisation, the government not only had to take over most of the debts of the existing railways, but a lot of jobs were also lost. Since losing a job in Japan is seen as a loss of honour, a large number of former workers committed suicide as a consequence. Also, many of the less frequented connections were completely abandoned. Today, the Japanese railways are still highly subsidised and charge high fares, but they are working reasonably well, especially the 'Shinkansen' high-speed connections.

There are two reasons why Japan is a special case and cannot easily be compared to other countries. Firstly, the structure of the country is such that it enables long-distance connections with high ridership basically along one long corridor. Secondly, the Japanese freeways have expensive tolls, and therefore the high railway fares are not a reason preventing usage of trains.

The Argentinean railways once extended over more than 40,000 km before they were privatised from 1991 onwards. The companies tried to focus on the profitable connections, and thus almost the entire railway system was shut down and 85,000 jobs were lost. Figure 3.5 shows the Argentinean railway system before privatisation and today. In addition to the loss of the rail network, the remaining infrastructure is at present in a poor condition, which regularly leads to terrible accidents such as the recent one in Buenos Aires on 22 February 2012 that left 49 people dead.

Figure 3.5

Argentinean Railway System Before Privatisation and Today

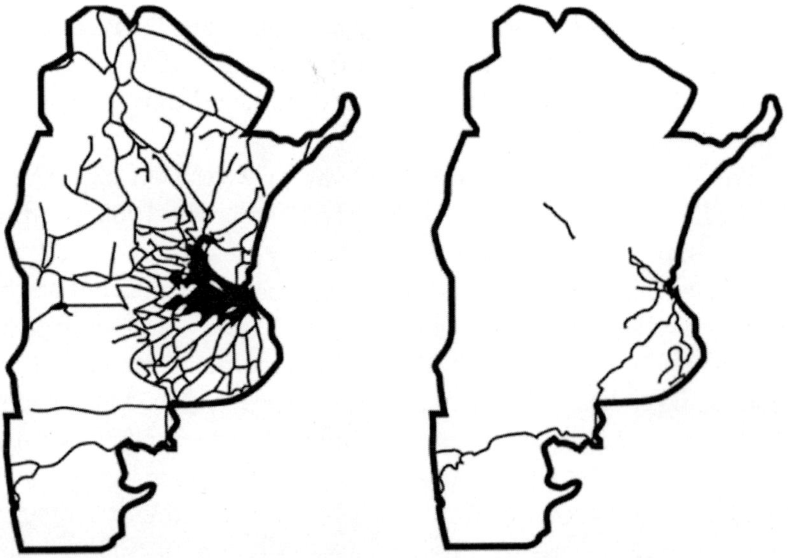

Source: Asociación del Personal de Dirección de Forrocarriles Argentions.

New Zealand (NZ) Rail was privatised in 1993 and sold to the US company 'Wisconsin central' for NZ-$ 328 million. The company made good profits, but did not invest sufficiently into the maintenance of the infrastructure. Therefore, the government bought back the infrastructure in 2003. In 2008, the government also bought back the railway operations—for NZ-$ 665 million alone.

There is a similar case in Eastern Europe. The Estonian government also had to buy back the railways from an American company at a huge loss—simply to keep it from completely breaking down.

The presented examples show that privatisation of a complete railway system might work for very few profitable connections, but it involves high risks, remains dependent on government subsidies and generally does not lead to a high quality rail network that can compete against other modes of transportation.

Privatising Infrastructure

The most famous case of railway privatisation is arguably Great Britain. Under the Thatcher government, the country started the privatisation process by splitting up the railways into different sectors. British Rail was formally privatised between 1994 and 1997, following the 1993 'Railways Act,' and split up into more than 100 companies. The infrastructure was operated by 'Railtrack,' which made huge profits over the first few years and was thus celebrated as a prime example for the success of privatisation. However, a few years later, several deadly accidents occurred, and it became obvious that 'Railtrack' had not sufficiently invested into the infrastructure. As a consequence 'Railtrack' went bankrupt, and the government had to reclaim the infrastructure in 2003. Now, 'Network Rail,' which is explicitly not oriented towards profit, operates the infrastructure. The government still has to invest huge amounts of money in order to bring the infrastructure back to a decent standard. Thus, the privatisation of the infrastructure alone is a complete failure.

Privatising the Transport Companies

While the infrastructure was re-nationalised, the rail traffic in Britain is still private, so the country can also be investigated as an example of the model of public infrastructure and private operating companies. Today, 25 different companies operate different train connections, and they all have different pricing systems and timetables not in accordance with each other. The service is generally described as very poor, but does this model at least pay off financially? The British Department of Transport commissioned the "Rail Value for Money" study, headed by Sir John McNulty (Department for Transport, 2011), which found that the British rail system is 40 per cent less efficient than other rail systems in Europe, thus costing both the customers and the tax payers over a third more compared to other European countries. Today, the government has to provide more subsidies to the private companies than it paid to British Rail before the privatisation. The inefficiency of the British system is mainly caused by the many interfaces and parallel structures caused by the fragmentation of traffic and to the costly bidding process. The costs of an average person-kilometre in Britain are almost twice as high as the costs in Switzerland, thus proving that private rail transport companies not only lead to bad service and a confusing system but also to significantly higher expenses.

Public-Private Partnerships

There is only one remaining model to bring private money into the railways: building of infrastructure as public-private partnerships (PPP). This has been attempted in Sweden, where the connection between Stockholm and the airport Arlanda has been built as a PPP project. Because the investor wants to earn money with the project, the fees for using the tracks on this connection are four times more expensive than the fees on public tracks. As a consequence, the connection from Stockholm to the airport is very expensive (similar to the Metro connection from Delhi centre to the Delhi airport) and does not get a high usage. Also, no long-distance trains stop at the airport, because the companies want to circumvent high costs. Therefore, the PPP infrastructure hardly fulfils its purpose to make people use railways instead of other modes of transport, and the revenues remain below expectations.

The Swiss railway system has also considered the involvement of private companies and commissioned a study, given that only a few examples exist where the PPP model has been tried for railway infrastructure so far. This study revealed that any potential savings made through PPP are eaten up by high transaction costs. This is mainly due to the necessity of having exacting contracts that have to mention several eventualities. The authors conclude that such PPP projects involve high public risks (Beckers *et al.*, 2010). Several PPP projects in Germany for building freeways support this view, as the costs for the public have been on average 30 per cent higher than if the government had built the infrastructure on its own (Tartler, 2012).

Public Railways Work: Switzerland

Switzerland is the only Western European country with no plans to privatise its railways. Through several plebiscites, the Swiss population decided to keep their railways public and implement the concept of 'Bahn 2000,' which has an IST as its backbone. This means that trains are optimally connected with each other and that all construction projects are aimed towards improvement of these connections and the expansion of the capacities of the railways. In this manner, the Swiss railways have minimised travel times between different stations without significant high-speed rail, which would have been much more expensive. Other modes of transportation such as buses in the mountains are part of this integrated system, and there is one unified pricing system for the complete public transit system in the whole country.

This approach is obviously very successful: in no other country do people use the railways as much as in Switzerland. The average Swiss goes more than twice the distance by rail than the average German—in an 8.6 times smaller country. At the same time, subsidies per person-kilometre in Switzerland are significantly lower than in other countries (Booz Allen Hamilton, 2006), so the public concept is cheaper for the state. As the usage of the Swiss railways is still further increasing, 'Bahn 2030' is supposed to continue further development and improvement of the railway system.

Privatisation on the Edge: Germany

When Germany became one country again in 1990, it had two railway systems: the 'Deutsche Bundesbahn' in the west and the 'Deutsche Reichsbahn' in the east. In 1993, the railway reform was passed by the German parliament. As a result, the entire debts of both systems were taken over by the government, and in 1994, the 'Deutsche Bahn AG' (DB AG) was founded as a new stock company.

DB AG has been constantly restructured since. It now has more than 500 sub-companies. Its main focus is no longer the operation of trains in Germany; it regards itself as a global player and has bought several international logistics companies. It is proud to be one of the biggest air cargo companies of the world—only outmatched by 'Deutsche Post AG/DHL,' the privatised German postal company. At the same time, the number of workers in the railway sector has been cut by half.

In 2005, plans to privatise DB AG became increasingly crystallised. Selling DB AG at the stock market was one of the central goals of the government. There was a long debate on which privatisation model to implement, while the option to keep it public was essentially excluded from the very beginning (Ibid). However, several polls saw about 70 per cent expressing preference to not privatise the railways at all.

To oppose this course of action, the alliance 'Bahn für Alle' ('railways for everyone') was formed in 2005 by environmental NGOs, globalisation critics and unions. Today, 20 organisations are members of the alliance. The alliance created strong political pressure against privatisation through public action, discussions, media and lobbying. As a result, the government continued delaying the privatisation plans and came up with increasingly complicated models to privatise certain parts of the system without others (mainly the infrastructure). In 2008, the government finally decided to sell off 24.9 per cent of the 'mobility' part of the DB AG at the stock market. The initial public offer was set for October 2008 but was called off just a few days before. The official reason for this was the stock market crash that would have led to small revenues. However, the reason was also partly due to insufficient maintenance coming to light at that time after a broken train axis and an almost-accident of a high-speed train.

Therefore, DB AG is still public today, although some of the regional rail lines are being operated by private companies. However, maintenance was cut significantly over the last 10 years in order to make the railways 'fit for the stock market.' Consequently, there are frequent technical problems: trains are often unpunctual, and there are no reserve capacities—parts of the system break down completely if there are any technical problems. Due to cost savings, Berlin City trains ('S-Bahn') are not working properly any longer with whole lines being shutdown for weeks. Officially, Germany has a public railway system, but it is essentially operated as a stock company. The grave results of this policy are clear.

How Can Railways be Financed?

As no privatisation model seems to lead to favourable results and governments usually claim not to have sufficient funds, how can a modern railway system be financed? The only remaining option is generating the money from those modes of transport that are less environmentally friendly such as air and road traffic. Taxing these modes of transport and using the money to build a more attractive and affordable railway system is a means of environmental and social politics.

References

Beckers, T., A. Brenck, J.P. Klatt, H. Sommer and T. Zimmermann (2010). *Eignung des PPP-Ansatzes zur Realisierung von Projekten im Bahnsektor sowie zur (Vor-)Finanzierung von ZEB- und Bahn 2030-Projekten.* Berlin/Bern, Eidgenössisches Departement für Umwelt, Verkehr, Energie und Kommunikation (UVEK), Bundesamt für Verkehr (BAV).

Booz Allen Hamilton (2006). *Privatisierungsvarianten der Deutschen Bahn AG "mit und ohne Netz" (PRIMON).* Berlin: Bundesministerium für Verkehr, Bau und Stadtentwicklung Bundesministerium der Finanzen. p.560.

Department for Transport (2011). *Realising the Potential of GB Rail.* Report of the Rail Value for Money Study. London: Department for Transport.

IFEU (2011). *UmweltMobilCheck-Wissenschaftlicher Grundlagenbericht.* Heidelberg Institut für Energie-und Umweltforschung Heidelberg gGmbH (ifeu).

IPCC (2007). *IPCC Fourth Assessment Report: Climate Change 2007.*

Kolodziej, A.M. Malow *et al.* (2009). *Daten zum Verkehr, Ausgabe 2009.* Dessau, Umweltbundesamt.

Tartler, J. (2012). "Konzerne ziehen Bund über den Tisch", *Financial Times Deutschland.* Hamburg, Financial Times Deutschland GmbH & Co. February 13.

4

ANJALI GOYAL

Strategies for Making Railways a Sustainable Transport in India

Sustainability in the Context of Railways

Railways are well established as a sustainable, environment friendly mode of transport. Empirical data vary from country to country, but broadly, travelling by rail is on average 3-10 times less CO_2 intensive compared to road or air transport (International Union of Railways, and Community of European Railway and Infrastructure Companies, 2008). Traffic carried by railways emits about 13.5 g of CO_2 per tonne kilometre, against an emission factor of about 135.9 g of CO_2 per tonne kilometre for heavy trucks.[1] However, fuel efficiency is not the only factor that defines sustainability. Sustainability has evolved into an expanded, multidimensional concept, covering not only economic viability, but also social and environmental sustainability. A lasting definition of sustainability was given by former Norwegian Prime Minister G.H. Brundtland: "Development that meets the needs of the present, without compromising the ability of the future generations to meet their own needs."

Economies like India and China face the challenge of balancing the objective of rapid growth to raise the living standards of vast sections of their population with the need to conserve limited resources like arable land, water, minerals and the environment. A sustainable development strategy requires energy conservation and environment friendly, efficient transportation. Herein lies the role of railways as the backbone for a sustainable transportation system. World over, governments seek to achieve goals of balanced economic and regional

1. Information obtained from unpublished material provided by World Bank office, New Delhi.

development, reduction in emissions and energy efficiency through expansion and technological upgradation of the rail sector.

The question is, as the fourth largest railway system in the world, traversing 65,000 route km, with a moderately widespread geographic outreach, carrying one billion tonnes of freight traffic and 8.2 billion passengers a year, can the railways claim pride of place as a sustainable transport in India?

The First Reality Check: Railways' Share in the Transport Market

Despite having the second densest railway network in the world at 20 km for every 1,000 sq km of land (after the USA), Indian Railways' (IR) share in passenger transport is less than 13 per cent. In terms of population coverage, however, IR is relatively low in comparison to comparable railway systems, at only 57 km per million population (Figure 4.1).

Figure 4.1

Population Coverage: Indian Railways in Comparison to World Railway Systems

(Rail route (in km)/million population)

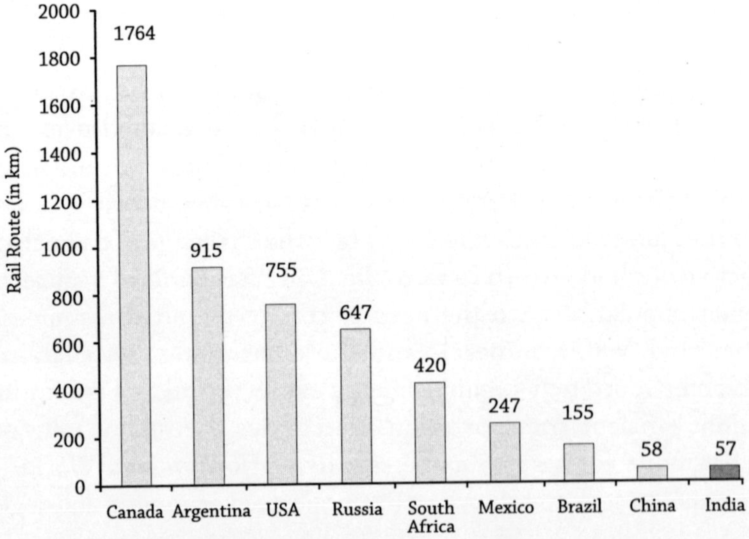

Source: Figure prepared by the author based on data obtained from following sources:
(i) *http://en.wikipedia.org/wiki/Rail_usage_statistics_by_country.*
(ii) *http://data.worldbank.org/indicator/IS.RRS.TOT.KM.*
(iii) *http://www.cia.gov/library/publications/the-world-fact book.*

IR's same network also carries 30 per cent of India's total freight cargo but ranks fairly low amongst similarly placed railway systems in terms of freight carried per route km (Figure 4.2).

Figure 4.2

Freight Carried: Indian Railways in Comparison to World Railway Systems

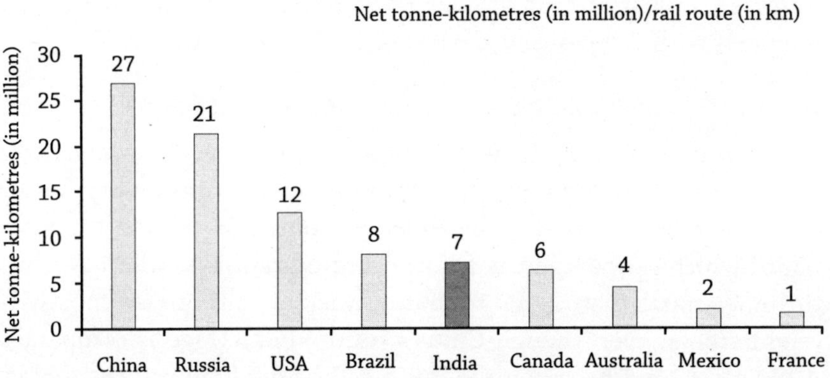

Source: Ibid.

Another Reality Check: The Economic Impact of Railways in India

Early railway lines in colonial India were patronised by Indians mainly because of their amazing speed, carrying capacity, and low fares and tariffs railways offered as compared to travel on roads and circuitous, slow moving riverine barges. Prior to completion of Bengal's 121 km Howrah-Raniganj Railway in 1855, it took two seasons to transport coal (Wolmar, 2014: 49; Srinivasan *et al.*, 2006: 16), whereas the trains moved larger volumes in a matter of hours. Similarly, fast and bulk, semi-trans-sub-continental rail movement of salt from coastal belts brought down salt retail prices for consumers by as much as 75 per cent (Donaldson, 2010). The dramatic impact of rail transport on the economy is reflected in empirical studies that suggest a social saving of 9 per cent of national income due to railways, based on the variation of freight rates between railways and bullock carts. These studies indicate that freight rates would have been higher by nearly 90 per cent in India if railways had not come (Hurd, 1983). These studies may not be a complete assessment of the impact of railways, as there is no way of assessing the social costs of congestion that would be involved in carrying the growing volume of passenger and freight traffic by roads and rivers in the absence of technologically advanced railways. Nevertheless, the saving in social costs in the early years of railways stands in sharp contrast to the relatively high logistics cost in India today, compared with developed countries. Logistics cost to GDP of India is as high as 14 per cent compared with 7-8 per cent in countries like the USA.

Why are Railways Not Able to Improve their Market Share?

The main reason is the way in which the economy grows in India. For example, take the case of coal, the mainstay commodity for any large rail freight system. India consumes only 554 million tonnes of coal of which 80 per cent is transported by railways, whereas China consumes more than 2,000 million tonnes of coal carried mostly by freight trains, even though China's route kilometrage is comparable to India's. China has acquired and used heavy haul rail technology faster and in a much more efficient manner than India or even the USA. Rail transportation of chemicals and steel in India is also limited compared to developed countries because of the smaller scale of manufacturing industrial base and its growth in India. This being the case, consumption of minerals like iron ore and coking coal is also too less for railways to look forward to. In more ways than one, railways in India are more sinned against than sinning, at least in respect to market share.

The rapid expansion of highways and expressways has steadily eroded railways' market share in freight and passenger movement. The rise in share of road traffic is propelled by marked improvement in road infrastructure and upscaling of motorised transport technology, yielding higher fuel efficiency and riding comforts.

Revisiting the Railways' Role as a Sustainable Transport

There can be no doubt that expansion of railways is a prerequisite for a subcontinent-sized country like India with an economy growing at over 7 per cent. India's hitherto rapid growth rate of more than 9 per cent is presently challenged by capacity limitations of the country's resources, infrastructure and environment. By 2020, India's total demand for power is projected to reach 1,870 terawatt hours, total vehicle fleet (2/3-wheelers + passenger vehicles + trucks) demand to reach 222 million, demand for cement to increase to 509 million tonnes and total floor space demand for residential and commercial buildings will touch 21 billion sq mt.[2] This is a typical case of unusually rapid economic growth, declining poverty, rising rate of urbanisation, a young mobile population in search of jobs and opportunities and a burgeoning middle class with aspirations on the one hand colliding with a lack of living space, transport infrastructural links, power and water supplies as well as shrinking land holdings and environmental degradation on the other.

India is at a stage of development where demand for transport grows linearly with GDP growth and rail transport is dominated by requirements of the primary sector. The geographic divide between sources of industrial raw materials and commercial/industrial activity centres make railways irreplaceable for nationwide transportation of bulk cargo like coal, mineral and non-mineral ores, building materials, food grains and fertilisers over medium and long distances. Coal is and will remain the mainstay of energy production in India for at least the next few decades. Transportation of 80 per cent of coal is by rail. IR's network has to create capacity to move coal to match projected demand of more than 1,250 million tonnes (MT) by 2025 (Planning Commission, 2006: 25), at an anticipated 8 per cent GDP growth. India is also weak in mineral wealth resources and will be increasingly dependent on import of coal and ores. IR has to gear up in order to enhance rail connectivity of all major ports and mines to the main network to carry coal and ore imports.

Railways are vital for balanced regional development. The high-capacity, all-weather features of railways make them an important link for integrating the economy. Transport occupies an important position in the multi-dimensional vulnerability index of India's population developed by Anu Kapur (2010). Ten per cent weightage has been given to connectivity of villages by pucca road and another

2. *Business and Economy* magazine, 1st March 2012, B&E indicators, p. 20.

10 per cent for rural urban distance. The lack of metalled road connectivity means households are deprived of basic health and education, and more time is spent in travel instead of on more productive activities.

The rural-urban distance implies lack of access to better services and facilities, less scope for participation in and utilising socio-economic activities that exist in urban areas.

With nearly 65 per cent of the population residing in rural areas, new rail lines are still required for disadvantaged regions to promote regional balance and inclusive growth. More than 50 per cent of India's population is below poverty line (BPL) and lower above poverty line (APL) income groups. Their travel budgets are small. Railways are a valuable, affordable means of transport for these millions. Trains are vital transport for the rural migrants who seek seasonal work in nearby urban townships or across the country in urban conglomerates. With the seasonal work over, they travel back to their rural habitations. The exodus towards rural areas during festivals and cropping season and the surge of traffic on passenger trains is well known.

Having established the need for railways expansion in the country, the question to be addressed is whether more expansion of railway capacity, in the business-as-usual mode alone, can make railways a sustainable transport.

The answer has to be evaluated on all dimensions of sustainability: economic, social and environmental. A sustainable railway will have to significantly increase its market share to be economically and socially viable. This will require triggering a decisive modal shift from road to rail. Making railways the preferred choice of transport would rest on making it more affordable and competitive than road while offering improved travel comforts, add-on services and flexibility. This requires induction of advanced rail technology in rolling stock, permanent way, signalling and train control systems to support higher speeds, capacity and riding comforts in railways services at economical costs. In the sections that follow, some of the strategies to achieve these goals are discussed.

Strategies for Making Railways a Sustainable Transport

Fast Track Completion of Dedicated Freight Corridors

While coal, heavy ores, food grains and fertilisers will mostly constitute railways captive bulk cargo, sustainability demands that railways make inroads into the dominantly road-bound commodities segment (Figure 4.3). Although rail transport costs are cheaper than trucks in India, modal shift in the case of containerised social goods and non-containerised general goods is not picking up much momentum at present. A major constraint faced by railways in this segment is providing assured transit time, available-on-demand facility and carrying capacity at competitive rates. Dedicated rail freight corridors will help cover this gap in freight services to force a modal shift in freight shipments in favour of railways.

Designed for double-stack container train operation, these corridors will provide seamless movement for freight trains on the densest freight movement routes by segregating passenger and freight movement on rail. Improved freight service features like fuel-efficient locomotives, lower terminal detentions and costs, higher average train speeds, heavy-haul trains carrying 6,000 to 8,000 tonnes or more trailing loads and reduced tare (unladen) weights of trains should help in time-sensitive, low-cost operations. The strategy should be to develop a symbiotic relationship with road transport. Strategically located logistics hubs can enable long haul by train and short-haul door-to-door connectivity by road, enabling overall sustainability for the future.

Build Railway Lines as Development Corridors

Transport systems have to be designed, developed and operated efficiently for sustainability. Railways are capital expensive. Economic viability dictates that railways be densely utilised. A predominantly rural population, seeking better jobs in growing urban centres, requires affordable railway services. Integrating social and economic viability requires that railways routes be developed as 'development corridors.' A classic example is the Delhi-Mumbai Industrial

Figure 4.3

Indian Railway's Freight Basket

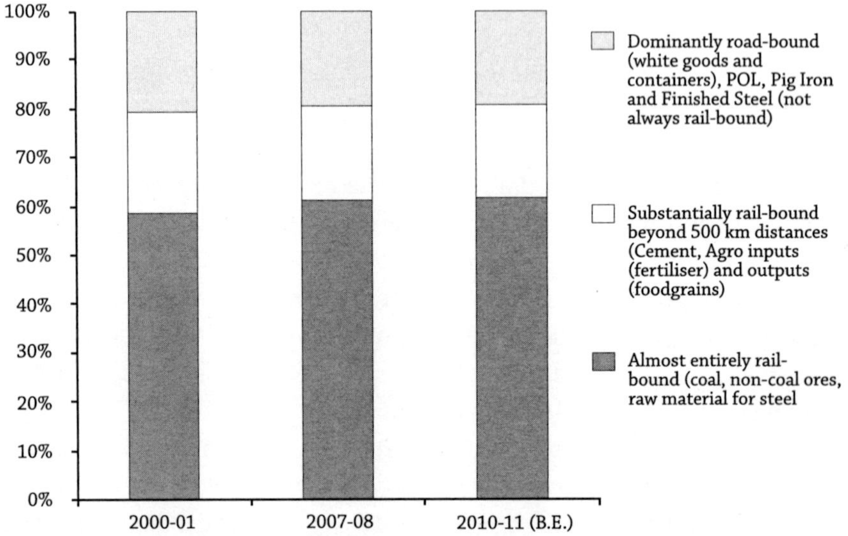

Source: Figure prepared by the author based on data obtained from Indian Railway Year Book 2001-02, 2009-10 and 2011-12.

Corridor (DMIC) being developed 150 km on either side of the western dedicated rail freight corridor. Intersecting seven states, this industrial corridor will develop 24 manufacturing cities covering manufacturing, information technology (IT)/IT-enabled service (ITES)-based activities, electronics and hi-tech industries, automobile units, agro-based industries, heavy engineering, metallurgy, pharmaceuticals, etc. These industrial clusters will form an organic relationship with the rail connectivity, with intermodal logistics support of ports, airports, feeder railways and highways and logistics hubs. This is the nation's first corridor being developed as an environmentally sustainable infrastructure, complete with planning for water harvesting, power and natural gas grid. It will directly benefit 355 million (30%) of India's 1,210 million population living in six states, namely Delhi, Haryana, Rajasthan, Madhya Pradesh, Gujarat and Maharashtra, through which this industrial corridor passes. Since the corridor covers Noida-Dadri complex too, Uttar

Pradesh with a population of 199 million will share the benefits. Similar 'development corridors' can be made along new/existing rail routes to enhance economic activity, leveraging rail connectivity and at the same time stepping up traffic potential for railways.

Raise Speed of Passenger Trains

Segregation of passenger and freight traffic on two of the busiest legs of the Golden Quadrilateral—eastern and western—will release capacity on existing corridors to run more frequent and faster passenger services. The railways are planning to increase train speed from 160 km/hr to 200 km/hr. Supplemented by very high-speed trains running at 300 km/hr on select, high-density passenger new routes like Delhi-Mumbai and Delhi-Chandigarh would make a significant intermodal shift in passenger transport possible. High-speed trains running on dedicated passenger tracks at 250 km/hr to 300 km/hr can serve as a transport cum logistics backbone for city clusters spanning across distances up to 1,500 km. This would enable deeper outreach of industry seeking new labour markets, rapid annihilation of distances to foster economic growth and an even spread of employment opportunities. This transport system is 10 times more fuel efficient than air, per passenger km. The economic value created by an efficient transport system is far greater than the profitability of operations.

Develop Advanced Rail Technology Residency[3]

Sustainable growth in the context of efficient, affordable rail transport systems will involve technology residency and development in local shores, under the protective umbrella of the government. This is what first world nations like the US, France, Germany and Japan have done for decades and is what is right now evolving dramatically, though somewhat controversially, in China. All these, however, need a clear national strategy and supportive national policy. Strategy should include: (a) government-nurtured sustained thematic research

3. This section is based on deliberations with: R. Sivadasan, former Financial Commissioner, Railways, and General Manager, Chittaranjan Locomotive Works, and Sujeet Mishra, Director (Electrical), Research Design and Standards Organisation.

ecosystems; (b) universities that create supply of high-quality human resources; (c) dedicated research labs to take over sensitive research; and (d) government bodies keeping the large picture in sight.

For example, when considering an ultra low-carbon transport mode like high-speed rail (HSR), it must also be ensured that HSR option itself remains sustainable in India. Under the present planning/approval processes, there is a tendency to simply treat HSR as another project for creation of infrastructure. The need to leverage technology acquisition and internalisation cannot be glossed over, and wearing components of the system, which call for periodic attention (continuous, hourly, daily and long intervals), cannot be done purely on annual maintenance contract basis. Dangerously wrong parallels get drawn with the airline industry, where it is thought that as fleet owner, one need not worry about maintenance. This approach disguise the fact that pre-flight checks are still done by the airlines and which survive because of a global, healthy and competitive maintenance, repair and overhaul (MRO) segment. But when it comes to advanced rail systems, pure economic considerations dictate the need for resident technology in the country (as realised by China). Big-ticket projects which fail to internalise and assimilate the technologies locally do not contribute in the recipient nation's developmental or wealth-creation process.

The slow pace of development in locomotive technology in India can be gauged by the fact that until the acquisition of electro-motive diesel (EMD) technology in mid-1990s, diesel locomotives were only being manufactured by American Locomotive Company (ALCO) technology, which incidentally wound up decades ago. The only noteworthy development in locomotive technology from the 1970s was the development of Co-Co trimount bogie, the basis of ubiquitous WDM2s (Indian railways' workhorse diesel locomotive) and WAM-4s (a form of electric locomotive). Another was Hitachi's hi-adhesion bogie of imported WAG-6C series (a series of electric locomotives), which, after initial hiccups, was successfully adopted on WAG-7 class electric locomotives and WDG-2 diesel locomotives. But these changes were not products of superior understanding of locomotive technology or system engineering approach *per se*. The approach has been to adopt better sub-systems instead of foreseeing and initiating development *ab initio*. Therefore, components (such as motors, compressors, brake-systems) were mere adoptions of existing products elsewhere in the world. However, this automisation and product-based designs and localisation was sufficient to lower cost of ownership because there are multiple vendors available in the country. In all spheres, prices came crashing down as soon as monopolies were done away with, and vendors of monopolistic products became aware that IR engineers have understood the technology sufficiently enough to develop second sources; this applied to all sub-systems, most notably to brake systems and compressors in new generation locomotives.

One successful transfer of technology (ToT) occurred when IR took Hitachi technology for the direct current (DC) traction motor in the 1980s. This motor has powered IR's quest to haul heavier, faster trains for at least 25 years. Initial ToT challenges were overcome and the motor went on to be highly successful. The motor was manufactured by Chittaranjan Locomotive Works and Bharat Heavy Electricals Ltd. (BHEL), which brought in multiple modifications to make the motor survive Indian operating and maintenance practices. The manufacturing of the motor gave fillip to several small companies which specialised in smaller parts of the motor. The design has been mastered by some other Indian companies in the private sector and enabled them to take business in repairs and component supplies to the global market. DC traction motors demanding higher maintenance are now fully maintainable and manufactured in the country. This has brought resilience in cost of operations.

It is important to understand subtle and not so subtle differences between aircrafts and rolling stock. In most of the products, there are two clear layers of components; one which change rapidly and the other which stay on. Jumbo-jets/Boeing's 747 took to wings in the 1960s and the celebrated U2 surveillance planes were designed in the 1950s. Both of them are still in active service. They did, however, undergo several retrofitments of sub-systems that have a small lifespan, like avionics or engine assemblies. Similarly, on the rolling stock, the mechanical framework represents a slower-to-change layer *vis-à-vis* power electronics and control components, and thus needs an upgrade in a framework of 5-10 years. Memories and processors undergo substantial change in a matter of years. These programmable platforms need IT-based tools, which are shared with commercial computing platforms like PCs running general operating systems like Microsoft products, which in turn undergo fundamental changes every few years. This keeps maintenance teams continuously on edge.

The demands of IR as a transporter are dynamic. This is reflected in motive power. Variants of imported platforms, permitting addition of coaches to existing trains without losing time, could be turned out given that IR had access to system integration information. This formed the basis of taking projects under the National Mission on Power Electronics (NaMPET)[4] to develop locomotive's uppermost layer of control, which integrates all sub-systems and defines locomotive's characteristics on open platforms, third-party development and operating systems. This has involved work in research labs and academia, and now needs to be taken forward if the cost of ownership is to be kept low. This demands elimination of complete dependence on manufacturer through the option of part insertion and part retirement, whereby a sub-assembly is retired without affecting the complete system—something successfully proven on aircrafts. This example indicates how important it is to understand the nuances of the need to have access to key components of technology.

Maintaining a fleet over its economic life is a tedious task, which can make or break an organisation, given the kind of financial exposure called for by such projects. As a buyer, at least two levels of backups should be created before multi-billion dollar commitments and commitments of an annual spending of thousands of crores of rupees are made. Failure to do so can be very costly.

Japan, France and Germany have been flag bearers of HSR because they created the technology. China today has gate-crashed

4. *www.nampet.org*

the elite club after taking technology from these countries. Academic/ research institutions with capability of mature technology uptake were involved to make possible true technology transfer.

India may choose a contractual model of HSR induction by making financial closure the only aim. Ignoring hard lessons learnt would make the system thus acquired end up enriching only the finance and technology provider (no matter how well-structured a deal, India would end up paying every rupee) and to keep the fleet afloat enormous funds would be needed after a decade or so.

Making India's rail system sustainable would require the following:

- Seek a national consensus that rail sector is driven by resident technology.
- If it is decided to acquire train-set technology, the aim should be not only residency of the initial technology, but also developments thereon to be resident within the country.
- Atomise the platform, i.e., break it down to components, for example, in energy-efficient electric locos/distributed propulsion train sets—bogies, current collection system, traction motors, converters, transformers, air supply systems, brakes, driver interfaces, etc. Decide which can be taken from Indian sources. These products can then be indigenously made with incremental inputs, for which India already has a robust industrial manufacturing base; further tie-ups can be encouraged. Almost all the leading world-class manufacturers of train sets/locomotives have already entered into similar tie-ups in China and South Korea and would be willing to enter into similar tie-ups with Indian manufacturers.
- Large and complex technology induction, such as for converters, should be entrusted only with IR production units or public sector undertakings like BHEL. ToT partners should be carefully chosen through rigorous competitive process that considers technology absorption suitability, capacity to invest and a genuine desire to be in rail component manufacturing.

- Government procurement rules for high technology products and critical software developments have to match the complexity of the acquisition when it comes to high-tech component and vehicle guidance system software, which first world countries do tend to hoard. Too much reckless competition in the name of annual contracts can kill tech-based original equipment manufacturer segments, as viable volumes are a must to sustain companies who want to be ToT partners.
- A national legislation like 'Buy India' Bill (similar to Buy America clause or the licensing system in China for inviting advanced technologies) may need to be moved in Parliament as a bill/act. This would also facilitate a spirited and open public consultation process on such sensitive policies.

Wider Range of Passenger Services with Public-Private Participation

Passenger rail services are viewed as slow, less frequent with congested terminals and trains, not clean and overcrowded. As income levels increase, passengers expect faster, higher-frequency train services with comforts in seating, on-board entertainment, choice of cuisine, cleanliness and hygiene, and assured timings. For railways to be a sustainable mode of transport in a fast growing economy, expansion of the infrastructure has to match the changing profile of demand for transport.

Railways face a growing opportunity in passenger transportation. Estimates of India's middle class population range from 30 to 300 million (Deutsche Bank Research, 2010; Kharas, 2011). Conservative estimates are at 100 to 160 million by Alam Srinivas (2008), Bijapurkar (2007) and National Council of Applied Economic Research (NCAER).[5] Based on NCAER data, Rama Bijapurkar (2007) indicates that 6 million households are rich and 75 million households constitute the consuming class. About 78 million households constitute climbers. Current estimates by NCAER

5. *articles.economictimes.indiatimes.com/.../28424975_1_middle-class-households-applied-economic-research.*

project middle class as 267 million by 2015-16. Railways can develop a bouquet of intermediate passenger services to match varying passenger expectations of a segmented passenger market.

New technology can be harnessed to reengineer coach space to carry more passengers, for example, seated instead of berths, double deck coaches, etc., to yield higher revenues from efficient coach floor space utilisation. This, accompanied with better available berth/seat km capacity sales and yield management, can increase fare box collections on every train trip.

Delivery of a passenger or freight service integrates a wide range of input services. New business models can be developed for PPP in rail passenger transportation by opening up a host of non-fare box business opportunities at the retail level. The station terminal itself can become a source of substantial revenues for investors, while providing much needed value-added services for passengers, ranging from restrooms to budget hotels and advertisement.

High-speed trains on select high-density routes offer a low-carbon option to attract passengers seeking ultra-fast transit with a high level of comfort and flexibility in services. All this will eventually lead to a shift of road traffic to rail, a step towards sustainable transport.

Upgrade Energy Efficiency of Railways

Large railway systems, like in Americas and Europe, continuously research new rolling stock, efficient operations, fuel efficiency, etc., in order to remain relevant in the transportation sector. Lighter, longer trains and a capacity to carry more freight/passengers in each train trip ensure price competitiveness. Added to this is the challenge of addressing carbon emissions in the transport sector. Notwithstanding the established fuel efficiency of railways as compared with road, there is a much greater scope for railways to address reduction in use of energy and resources and improve its position on the sustainability index.

Approximately 85 per cent of total energy consumed by the rail sector is used directly for rail traction. Energy efficiency thus offers a powerful, cost-effective tool for achieving a sustainable future. Three key efficiency measures on overall train energy consumption are: improving the efficiency of the traction system, reducing train mass and reducing train running resistance (friction and drag). A reduction of mass by 1 tonne/coach can lead to a 1 per cent drop in energy consumption. A 10 per cent reduction in air drag reduces energy consumption by 6 per cent (Network Rail, 2009). Fuel efficiency can be enhanced through upgradation of technology to reduce traction system losses, rolling stock designed for higher seating and tare weight reduction through appropriate utilisation of lighter material like composites. Improved space utilisation would result in a reduction in energy per seat km. Efficient driving strategies would reduce traction energy use.

Apart from this, there is considerable scope to address emissions resulting from construction, maintenance and decommissioning of rolling stock; energy consumption/emissions from construction of new infrastructure; etc. New manufacturing units, maintenance facilities, freight and passenger terminals, etc., can be more efficiently designed to minimise land use. Vertical space offers considerable untapped potential.

Proactive National Policy on Railways

Concerns for a sustainable future are driving governments to legislate on not just fuel efficiency and carbon emissions, but also on topics such as noise pollution, accidents and other externalities of the transport sector. Environmental legislation will drive development of technology towards a sustainable transport system. Railways as a sustainable transport will require land to expand coverage; technological upgradation to increase capacity, speeds and comfort in order to attract passengers and freight customers; PPPs for better services at the retail level; and funds. National policies and legislations will have to play a pivotal role in the associated socioeconomic decision making.

- Taxes and incentives: A stated policy/legislation on incentives for investment in railway sector will attract private funding to expand infrastructure and R&D in rail sector. Government interventions such as incentives for travel by environmentally friendly transport modes like railways would help in the modal shift towards rail. Funds for rail sector could also be generated through sin taxes on more polluting industries, activities and even socially undesirable consumption.

- HSR is very capital intensive. Even rich economies like the US and the UK seek national consensus and legislation for introducing such expensive projects. A national consensus and Act of Parliament can help position HSR as an altogether differentiated mode of transport bracketed with airlines. Without this, doubts will always be raised at such a high-cost infrastructure, ignoring the multiplier impact of HSR on economic and industrial activity, high-skill jobs, urbanisation and efficient low-carbon transportation.
- Land is increasingly becoming an emotive issue. The inherent advantage of railways is higher throughput of passengers and cargo per hour than a road of the same width. Added to that, railway tracks occupy less land space than a two-lane highway. A typical passenger railway carries 2.83 times as many passengers per hour per metre width than road.[6] In the case of HSR, the ratio is even more stark. Heavily patronised services like Shinkansen carry 20,000 passengers per hour per direction. A national policy on transport can help rationalise acquisition of land to conserve arable land and minimise displacement.
- PPP: PPP policy should cover not only the selection of PPP partner, but also business models, revenues share agreements, user charges, etc. PPP entails public sector functions being pursued in partnership with the private sector. Issues to be decided include: Are government accounting standards appropriate for PPP? Can legitimate commercial interests run into conflict with public audit? Can PPPs be competitive on government procurement rules? Accounting principles that will apply for PPP

6. *http://railsystem.net/highspeedrail.htm*

ventures in a transport public utility will have to be clearly announced before, and not after, transactions are made. Legitimate commercial interests of all stakeholders including government and end users will have to be equally addressed in an objective manner. This would build investor confidence and sustainable PPPs in railways.

References

Bijapurkar, Rama (2007). *We are Like that Only*. India: Penguin Books.

Deutsche Bank Research (2010). *The Middle Class in India. www.dbresearch.com*

Donaldson, Dave (2010). "Railways and the Raj: The Economic Impact of Transportation Infrastructure". *http://econ-www.mit.edu/faculty/ddonald/papers*

Hurd, John II. (1983). "Railways", in Dharma Kumar (ed.), *Cambridge Economic History of India—Volume II*. Cambridge: Cambridge University Press.

International Union of Railways, and Community of European Railway and Infrastructure Companies (2008). *Rail Transport and Environment, Facts & Figures*.

Kapur, Anu (2010). *Vulnerable India—A Geographical Study of Disasters*. New Delhi: Sage Publications.

Kharas, Homi (2011). *The Emerging Middle Class in Developing Countries*. Washington, DC: Brookings Institution.

Network Rail (2009). *Comparing Environmental Impact of Conventional and High-Speed Rail*. London: Network Rail.

Planning Commission (2006). "Coal Vision 2025", *Integrated Energy Policy Report of Expert Committee*. New Delhi: Planning Commission.

Srinivas, Alam (2008). *The Indian Consumer—One Billion Myths One Billion Realities*. John Wiley & Sons.

Srinivasan, Roopa, Manish Tewari and Sandeep Silas (2006). *Our Indian Railway: Themes in India's Railway History*. New Delhi: Foundation Books.

Wolmar, Christian (2010). *Blood, Iron and Gold: How the Railroad Transformed the World*. London: Atlantic Books.

5

ANSHUL GUPTA

Network Based Intelligent and Safe Train Control and Management System

Introduction

With constraints in line capacity and cases of safety breach due to staff failure on Indian Railways (IR), IR is looking for substantial improvement in their signalling and safety systems through adoption of modern technologies at optimal cost. In this effort, it is pertinent to identify the gaps in the present system and introduce technology, which can not only support legacy systems but is also able to integrate with new signalling and telecommunication systems of IR.

Any system derives its inherent features from the process it follows during its creation and architectural design. Cases in point are world-class high-rise buildings and atomic power plants. Nothing could have come, had an incremental approach been followed, without following a path of 'process-based integrated architect' principles. On IR so far, there has been no concept of 'process-based architect' because it has not yet been recognised that railways are in need of such concepts. It is now high time that railway signalling and telecom systems are given their due place of being an integrating 'process-based architect' of a modern railway network.

This paper aims to explain comprehensive network solutions that can be built using RailTel Corporation of India Limited's massive information and communication technology (ICT) infrastructure to achieve the objectives of this important mission of the Ministry of Railways.

Present Communication Systems in Railways

Indian railways has one of the largest and busiest rail networks in the world, transporting over 8 billion passengers and more than

900 million tonnes of freight per year. It is the world's largest utility employer, with more than 1.4 million employees. The railways traverse the length and breadth of the country, covering 6,909 stations over a total route length of more than 63,327 km. IR is divided into 16 zones, which are further sub-divided into divisions. Each of the 16 zones is headed by a General Manager (GM) who reports directly to the Railway Board. The zones are further divided into divisions under the control of Divisional Railway Managers (DRM).

To support this extensive rail network in the world, Indian railways have deployed various communication systems for its signalling and administrative requirement. The following independent telecom modules/systems/technologies are in use currently for various train operations and administrative purposes: optical fibre cable (OFC), quad cable, IR's over head (OH) alignment, Bharat Sanchar Nigam Limited (BSNL)'s OH, analogue MW/UHF, digital MW, 25W vehicle health monitoring (VHF) sets, mobile train radio communication (MTRC)/Global System for Mobile Communication-Railways (GSM-R), satellite, Synchronous Transport Module (STM)-4, multiprotocol label switching (MPLS)-IP, railway exchanges, mobile closed user group (CUG). These systems are being used to provide various signalling, administrative and commercial applications.

Safety Gaps in the Network Infrastructure

For any railway system the world over, telecom infrastructure must consist of:

- Fixed telecom infrastructure: Mostly OFC-based in the back haul, supported by OFC/Cu-based access network.
- Wireless network: Previously, railways used to have walky-talky as base support, but now for increased efficiency and productivity needs, global system for mobile communications—railway (GSM-R) or Tetra—is being used so that a wireless network supports communication with train for tracking and control.
- Broadband network: Of late, data needs have increased tremendously due to higher safety and passenger comfort

needs like communications-based train control (CBTC) and broadband on trains. This is back hauled on OFC-based core network.

- Long distance network: Large railways in particular need reliable and continuous long-distance networks. This is achieved using OFC back haul.
- Internet Protocol (IP) network: This is today's requirement for railway networks, which is achieved using next-generation technologies. All dispersed elements of train operations are made IP addressable, for increased safety and efficiency.

Considering the gaps in Indian railways, it is very clear that many of the above-mentioned networks do not exist, or if these exist, they are in the form of localised systems. However, with the vast potential of modern telecom infrastructure of RailTel's OFC-based next-generation network, one can easily create each of these networks and integrate spread-out elements. In this way, they can be made intelligent. Once RailTel's OFC platform is used to network them, there is no doubt that IR's mission of a true enhanced safety and security in train operations is not far away, by incremental investment only on safety electronics like automatic train control system, signalling track/rolling stock sensors. Here, the network shall be based on layered architecture with different layers providing various quality of service (QoS) and type of services.

Futuristic Network for Indian Railways

Present Domain of Services on Indian Railways

For operational excellence and safety ecology, Indian railways have accepted that it needs several ICT systems. Presently, the IT applications in IR operate in a limited manner and that too in isolation from each other (Table 5.1). Since they are not integrated on a common platform, the intended objective to achieve excellence, efficiency and fail-safe operations have not been achieved.

Table 5.1

IT Applications in Indian Railways

System	*Application*				
Operations	Crew management	Centralised train control (CTC)	Freight operations information system (FOIS), station management, parcel management		Train planning and tracking
Customer relationship management	Market research	Passenger reservation system (PRS)	Call centre	Customer data base	Customer service
Data capture	Radio frequency identification (RFID), fixed and mobile terminals	Supervisory control and data acquisition (SCADA) system	Data loggers		On-board hand held terminals
Maintenance/ Procurement	Asset planning	Asset performance monitoring system	Infrastructure management information system (MIS)	e- Procurement	Asset life cycle management
Business support systems	Human resources management	Procurement and contract management	Cash flow management	Integrated logistics management	Litigation management
Data processing systems	Train running, train tracking, payment gateways				
Safety	Automatic warning system (AWS)	Training protection and warning system (TPWS)	Global system for mobile communications – railway (GSM-R)	Anti-collision device (ACD)	Safe coaches

Source: Centre for Railway Information Systems.

In any developed railway system across the world, the systems work on an integrated multilayered ICT platform. At present, India has a number of these systems or processes but working in silos independently from each other, resulting in information of one department pertaining to operations and safety being integrated with another department's process/action. For example, track health monitoring does not know about rolling stock health monitoring or signalling, etc., but they often counteract each other.

What is to be Done?

The answer lies in creating new processes/systems, adopt integrated train operations, control and safety systems which have all field elements, and train-borne elements networked on a common ICT platform to create a safety ecology. This can be achieved only by adopting a generational-change approach and inducting suitable modern rolling stock, railway signalling, telecom and train control systems which can support:

- Train operation/control.
- Safety systems like training protection and warning system (TPWS), anti-collision device (ACD), European train control system (ETCS).
- Commercial application: ticketing.
- Operation support system: centralised train control (CTC), European rail traffic management system (ERTMS), track management system (TMS), freight operations information system (FOIS), etc.
- Passenger information system: centralised auto announcement, display boards, coach guidance systems.
- Data network: Railnet, management information system.
- Administrative needs: digital exchanges.

The basic aim of such an intelligent networked safety train control system is that it should:

- Enable dispatchers to look ahead in time, including drivers.
- Identify in advance where trains should meet and pass, and which trains should take sidings.

- Allows maintainers to see and select best 'blocks' for maintenance.
- Enable feedback provided by the intelligent networked system.
- Allow system, rather than local, optimisation.

Once that is achieved, India can successfully move towards:

- Automatic train control system and automatic train management system to take care of signal passed at danger, head on/rear on collisions in block sections, train parting, level crossing gate accidents, rail fracture, flat wheel, axle problems, etc.
- Use of OFC-based sensing system for detecting the presence of flat wheel, dislocation of track, rail clip removal, fractured rail, obstruction of the track, etc.
- Use of modern ICT systems to integrate all elements of train operations and monitoring and disseminating train running information.
- Provision of electronic surveillance to take care of any miscreant activity infringing the rail track or its assets/ dwellings endangering the rail track safety.
- Building of rolling stock ready with automatic train control (ATC) and automated track monitoring system (ATMS).
- Development of a people's rail portal for all its travel needs, freight transport, etc. (including train improvements like airlines have done, i.e., cloud-based ticket booking, check in, train information systems, etc.).

The aim is to make an integrated system as conceived in Figure 5.1.

Figure 5.1

Network-centric Intelligent Rail Safety Management Systems

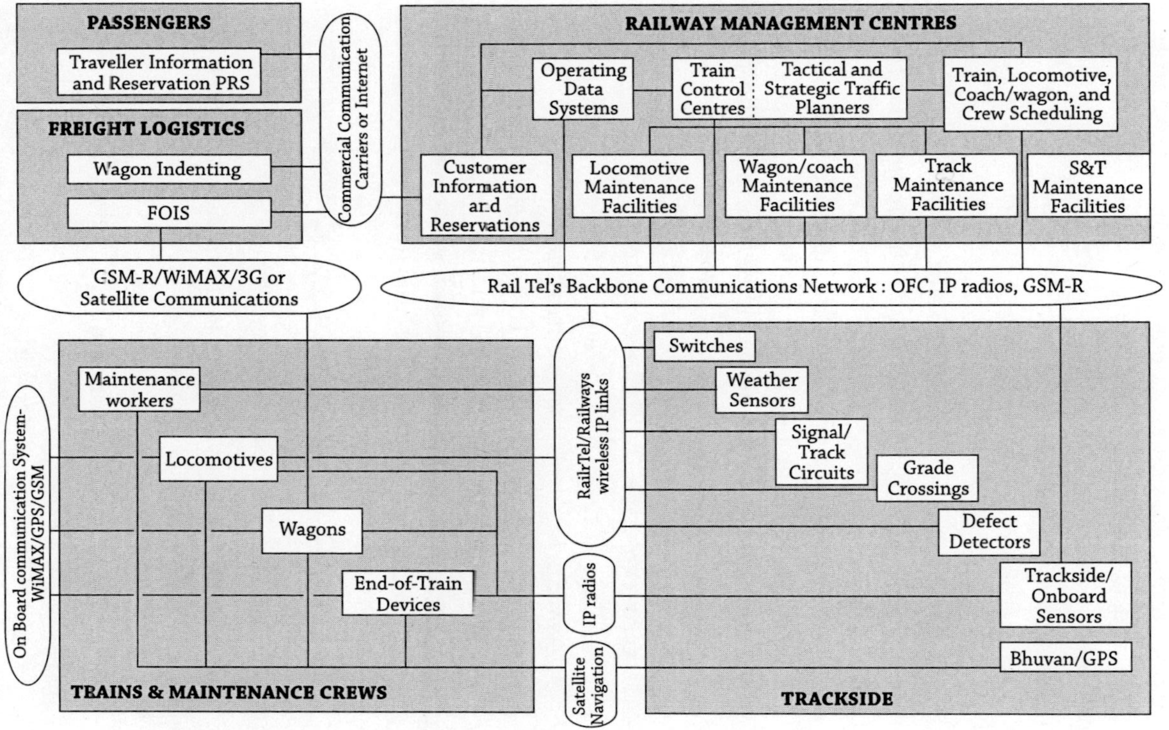

Source: Proposal to High Level Safety Committee by Rail Tel, January 2012.

As can be seen from the figure, all elements of railways have been networked on a multilayer telecom platform, such as (a) customer-centric systems: passenger, goods, train information; (b) railway control and management centres; (c) track side elements of all departments; and (d) train maintenance and overhauling support centres.

Future Network Requirement

Considering the above applications and spread of network, the following needs to be ascertained in the proposed/future core network:

- Development of interfaces to integrate with present/legacy systems (both analogue and digital).
- Fixed and moving network elements in the field/office/depots have to be made IP addressable.
- Integration of new ICT carrier technologies such as long-term evolution (LTE), WiMax, etc.
- Multipath resilient and reliable network, capable of working even during disasters/eventualities.
- Capable to provide end-to-end data communication for safety, security and general applications.
- Capable for quad play (voice, data, video and mobility), including encryption for mission critical operating and safety-related operations.
- IPv6 ready network.

Proposed Network Topology

Considering the above requirements, the whole network should include the following (see Figure 5.2):

- OFC-based basic infrastructure.
- Dense wave division multiplexing (DWDM) based core transport layer.
- Packet transport network (PTN) based aggregation service layer.
- Local OFC access network.

Figure 5.2

Proposed IT Network for Indian Railways

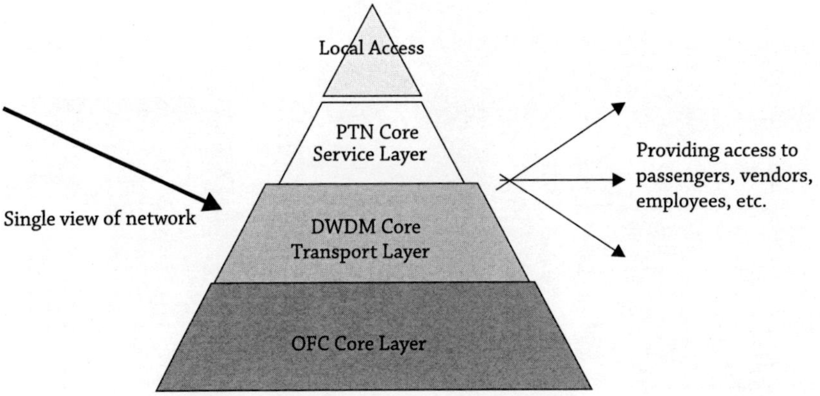

Source: Gupta, Ansul (2012). "Railway Security in India: PRISM", *Institution of Railway Signal Engineers (IRSE) News* 181: 6-10, September, London.

Network Architecture

RailTel proposes building the entire network based on a three-layered architecture on top of its existing OFC network. The OFC needs to be augmented through incremental fibre to cover all physical locations including all tracks, sheds, railway offices and stations (Figure 5.3).

Core layer shall be a dual segment architecture built in a ring topology connecting railway board, network operation centres, zonal railway headquarters, Research Design and Standards Organisation (RDSO), central training institutes, etc. This layer shall be built with self-healing multipath redundant high capacity back haul system. Here, there shall be two segmented sub-layers in core back haul, one for safety-oriented systems and modules and the other for passenger information and administrative functions.

Aggregation layer shall interconnect divisional offices, control offices, stations and major installations such as centralised traffic control (CTC), route relay interlocking (RRIs), maintenance and overhauling depots/sheds, passenger reservation system (PRS) control centres and centralised passenger information system (PIS) centres. Here also, it shall be configured in multipath ring topology to

Figure 5.3

Network Topology for Integrated ICT Platform for Operations and Safety Excellence on Railways

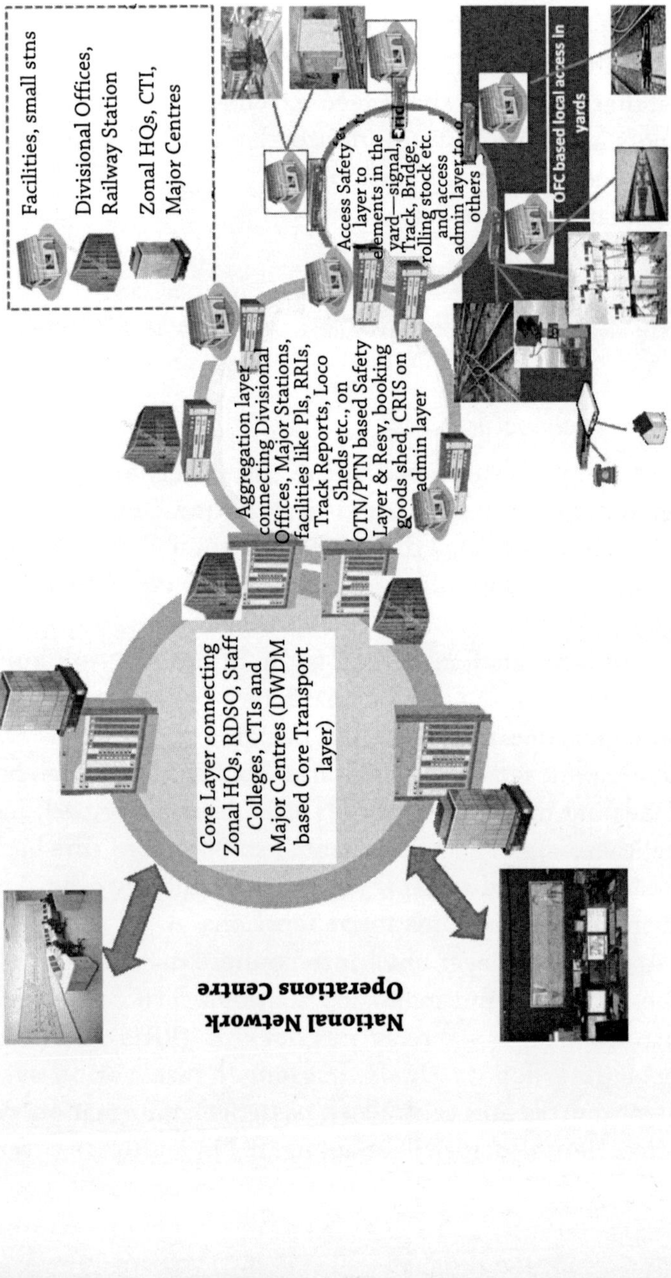

have best possible fault tolerance. There shall be two sub-layers here, one for safety installations/systems and the second for information and administrative installation/systems.

Access layer from each of the aggregation points/installation at a station, divisional office, PIS centre, PRS centre, goods shed, RRI or CTC: There shall be dedicated OFC-based access layer, overlaid by a radio-based link (GSM-R/LTE link for rolling stock based installation). This shall need extensive OFC laying in each yard, depots and stations to connect each and every independent element dispersed in the yard/station/depot using a ring topology for path redundancy (Figure 5.4).

Segmented Topology for Safety and Non-safety Applications

Safety systems and modules need different design in view of fail safety feature requiring nearly 99.99 per cent service level agreement (SLA). This is achieved through multipath redundancy. In developed railways, generally two fibres are laid, one on either side of the track. However, RailTel's vast network can provide a much better option of alternative multipath redundancy, thus taking care of common cause failure which may affect both the paths, in case OFC is laid on either side of the same track, thus guaranteeing better SLAs and fault tolerance. GSM-R or LTE–railway (LTE-R) as it is developed can then be overlaid on this OFC aggregation cum access safety layer to communication with on-board safety systems like automatic train control/training protection and warning system (ATC/TPWS) or ACD. The other elements like track, bridge, over head electrification (OHE), signals and level crossings can also interact with the on-board ATC/TPWS to rule out many possibilities of unsafe conditions including collisions, derailments, train parting, rail fracture and bridge integrity. The multipath redundancy for safety data traffic is achieved through route diversity along the natural rail routes.

OFC network has another property: it is sensitive to acoustic signals. Different acoustic signals signify different incidents, and based on a fail-safe sensor integrated with OFC system, fibre sensors can be used for a wide range of high-value applications.

Figure 5.4
Ring Topology

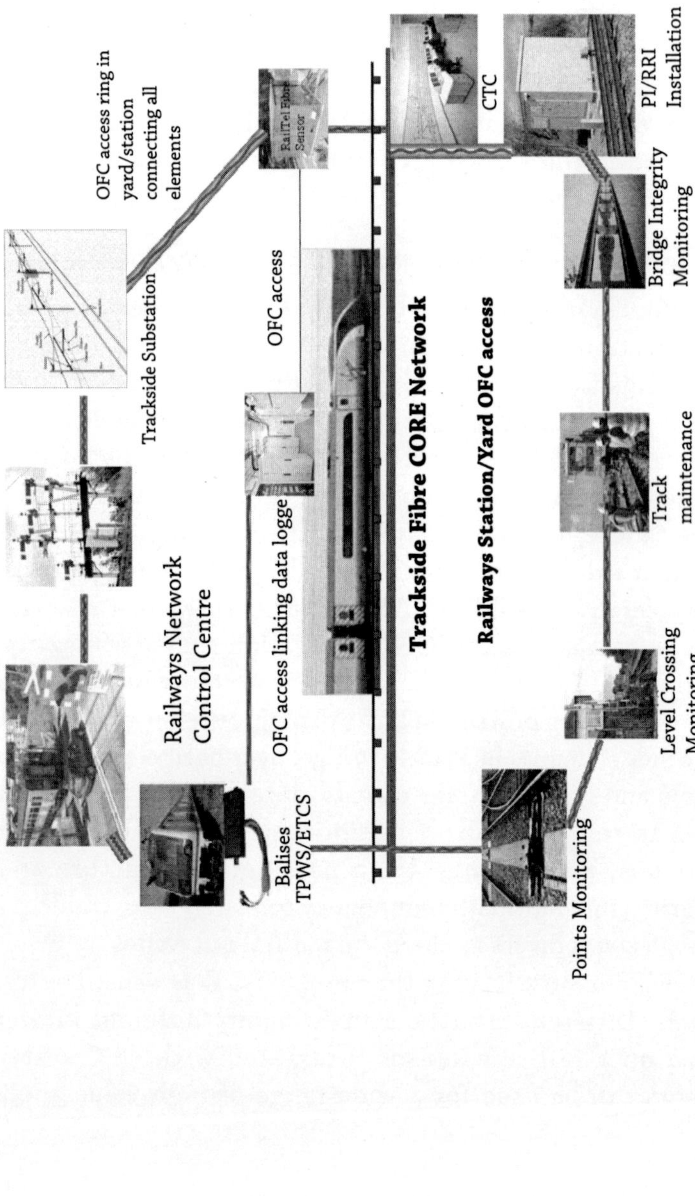

Examples include the detection of copper cable theft and other criminal activity; the detection of terrorist activity, for example, by placing an explosive device on or near the track; remote condition monitoring of points, damage to track, and rolling stock, for example, flat wheel detection; improved safety for trackside workers, by identifying what may be unscheduled work, where trains have not been suspended; early warning of hazards, for example, landslides and collisions involving bridges; and more accurate information on train location, and likely time of arrival for passengers and staff. As these applications are software based, the incremental cost is considerably less than the initial deployment, further strengthening what is usually already a very compelling business case. Similarly, it can be used for train actuated warning devices as well. Further, as it is known that a signalling system's most important component is detection or tracking of the location of trains, OFC network has another advantage in carrying out train detection. In conventional system, it is carried out using track circuits that split the track into 'blocks' and each block has associated signalling controlling access to the block. However, OFC-based sensors can provide an intelligent replacement without any visible track device. Network rail in the UK and a few other railways have started adopting such OFC-based sensors in a big way to leverage full potential of OFC network even for train operations, safety and security therein (Figure 5.5).

Thus, the following can be achieved in true sense using our vast OFC network:

- Network-based modern safety systems for train operations on pan India basis.
- Centralised train control systems with central network operations centre (NOC) using data loggers.
- Integrated safety and security systems.

Administrative and Passenger Information Sub-layer

RailTel's core and aggregation IP network can integrate various passenger information interfaces with operational data retrieval modules on this sub-layer to provide an integrated passenger information system on passenger reservation system, anywhere

Figure 5.5

Level Crossing Gate Warning System Using OFC-based Sensors

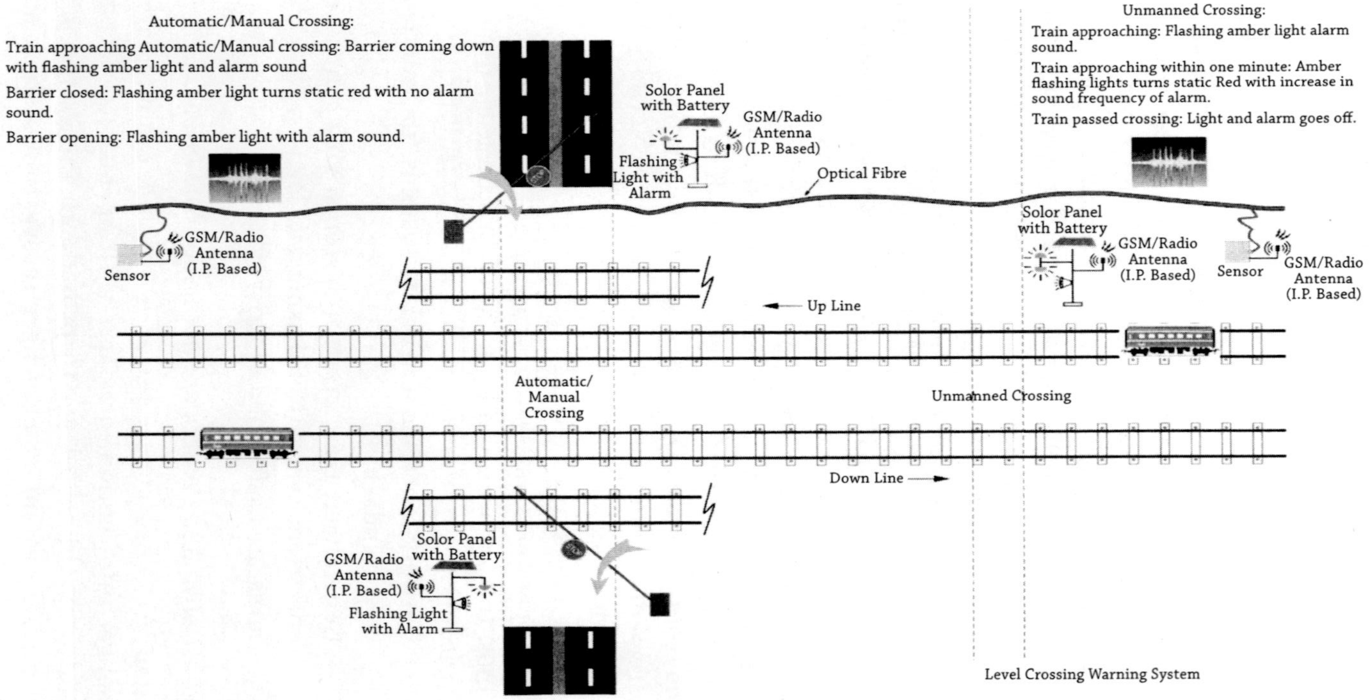

ticketing, train running information (fixed as well as on board), freight/parcel tracking system, journey planning, on-board entertainment system, railways internal management system, etc. Thus, another integrated sub-layer can provide:

- Integrated network enabling triple play services for communication between administrative staff/offices.
- Integrated network for all commercial applications like PRS, unreserved ticketing system (UTS), FOIS.
- Data/voice communication for staff on board and stations for commercial purpose.
- Passenger broadband and information services on stations/ on-board trains and through portal.

Summing Up

Traffic engineering features within the mesh network to be deployed by RailTel will ensure low latencies and high network uptime. Most of the core link can be set up by using RailTel's existing network to lower the cost of development, and by providing Indian railways with robust and fail-proof communication infrastructure along with better manageability.

The access network at offices/stations can be on LAN-based systems with IP version 6 (IPv6) support. However, for on-board coverage, the access can be provided by deploying LTE/GSM-R based system so as to enable sensors, data loggers, video surveillance cameras, handheld devices, etc., to access the service layer on the section as well as platform/shed areas. This will enable all the applications/services to be delivered in an integrated manner on a networked environment leading to a new safety regime, which will be truly fail-safe train operations.

6

ANURADHA SHUKLA

Road Traffic and Air Pollution in Delhi

Introduction

Transport is a key and crucial element in infrastructure needed for the developmental process, and roads are the dominant mode of transportation in India. Increasing urbanisation coupled with conglomeration of commercial and industrial activities have caused tremendous pressure on the existing transport system in India. Although transport makes a significant contribution to the national economy and to the quality of life, adverse effects of transport on the environment include emissions of greenhouse gases (GHGs), air pollutants, noise and damage to both the natural and built environment.

There has been a tremendous increase in the number of motor vehicles in Indian cities. This growth is expected to continue in the coming years also. Large cities, particularly the metros, have a higher concentration of motor vehicles than smaller towns. Indian roads are congested, even though the vehicle ownership rates are much lower in India as compared to the developed countries, and traffic congestion is very severe. The congestion results in crawling traffic, an increasing accident rate, fuel wastage and environmental pollution. Dramatic growth in vehicle ownership during the past decade has reduced the peak hour speeds to 5-10 km an hour in the central areas of major cities.

Urban transport is one major cause of air pollution in Indian cities adversely affecting the health of people and their quality of life. Due to the lack of integrated land use and transport planning in most of the cities today, there are a plethora of personalised modes and a scarcity of public transport modes. In a study carried out by the Central Road Research Institute (CRRI), pollution loads in major cities have been estimated. Delhi has the highest pollution load compared to any other city in the country. The exhaust from the tailpipe of automobiles has contributed much towards the deterioration in air quality in Delhi, leading to health and respiratory diseases.

Population and Vehicles Growth in Delhi

Delhi, the capital city of India, is located in the north, shares its border with the states of Uttar Pradesh and Haryana and has an area of 1,483 sq km. Its maximum length is 51.90 km and greatest width is 48.48 km. The 2001 Census recorded a 13.85 million population in the city with 3.85 per cent annual growth rate and a decennial growth rate of 47.02 per cent during 1991-2001. The population growth trends from 1951 to 2001 for major metropolitan cities of India are shown in Figure 6.1. It can be seen that Delhi is very rapidly growing with an average annual population growth rate of about 4.5 per cent,[1] followed by Bengaluru (3.38%) and Mumbai (2.68%). The total population of Delhi accounts for 1.34 per cent of India's population whereas in area, it is only 0.05 per cent of the total area of the country. The population of national capital territory of Delhi as per 2011 Census Provisional Population Totals is 16.75 million, of which 97.5 per cent is the share of urban population. Delhi is expected to become the third largest populated city in the world by the year 2015.

With the increase in population, income levels and economic activities, travel demand has increased manyfold. Inadequate public transport and the easy availability of financing facilities for private vehicles have resulted in increased vehicle ownership and their usage. Further, the changes in urban form and structure in terms of land use, density of population and concentration of activities have changed the travel pattern. In other words, traffic problems are increasing in the city in general, the situation is becoming complex particularly in core areas of the city, and this has increased the pressure on the existing road network.

The automobile population in India has increased from a mere 0.3 million in 1951 to more than 88.57 million in 2006. Registered

1. India has recorded national average growth rate of 2.1 per cent per annum.

Figure 6.1

Growth of Population in Metropolitan Cities of India

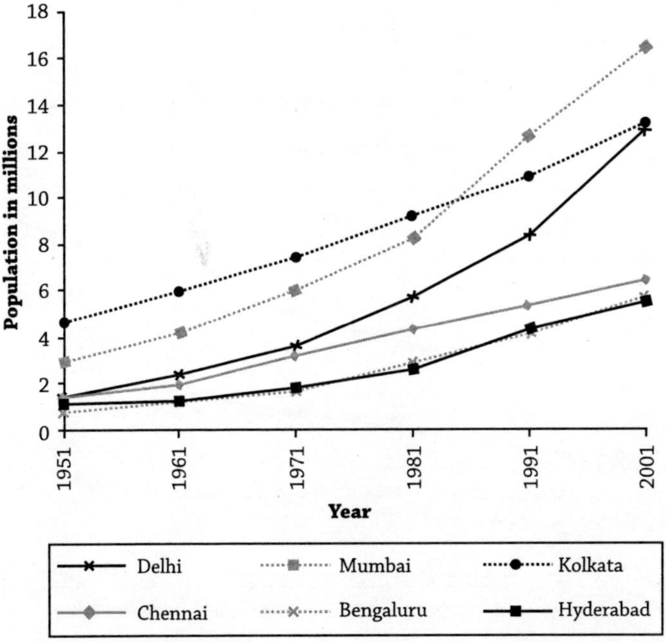

Source: Central Road Research Institute, 2002.

two-wheelers constitute nearly 70 per cent of the vehicle population in almost all the cities. Due to higher income levels and greater needs for mobility in the urban areas, more automobiles are owned and operated in such regions: more than 90 per cent of the automobiles are located in urban centres. This trend is observed to be changing in the recent past mainly due to the development of better quality road network connecting rural areas and richer communities of rural areas opting for automobiles.

Delhi has more than 5.63 million total registered vehicles, as per 2008 (more than 12% of India's automobile population) with a predominance of two-wheelers and cars as shown in Figure 6.2. Further, motor vehicles in Delhi have grown to a greater extent than the road network, thus leaving a large shortfall in the capacity required to carry the motor vehicles plying in the city. It can also be observed from the figure that on an average, about 1000 new vehicles are added on Delhi roads every year, resulting in extreme congestion, ever slowing speeds, increase in road accidents, fuel wastage and environmental pollution.

Figure 6.2

Growth Trends of Motor Vehicles in Delhi

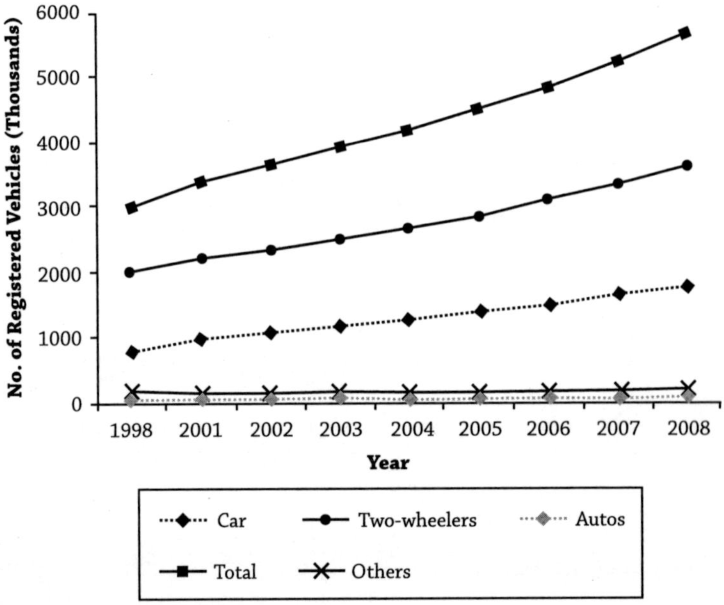

Source: Shukla and Alam, 2010.

Motor Vehicular Emissions

Emissions from motor vehicles with gasoline- or diesel-powered engines can be identified and categorised into three main types: crankcase, fuel system and exhaust emissions. Crankcase emissions account for roughly 20 per cent of the hydrocarbon (HC) emissions of uncontrolled vehicles. In new vehicles, this is prevented by closing the crankcase vent and avoiding its exposure to the ambient air. The locked-up gases of the crankcase are re-circulated to the intake manifold. Crankcase emissions from diesel vehicles are noted to be marginal.

Exhaust emissions from road traffic contain the products of fossil fuel combustion. These emissions consist mainly of water vapour and carbon dioxide (CO_2), emitted by the complete combustion of fossil fuel. It is difficult to achieve complete oxidation in practice, so carbon monoxide (CO) and HC are emitted as products of incomplete combustion. In addition, nitrogen in the air combines with oxygen in the combustion chamber and results in nitrogen oxides (NO_x). The primary emission is nitric oxide, but this is largely oxidised further to nitrogen dioxide when in contact with the atmosphere. Particulate matter (PM), which consists of solid carbonaceous compounds, is also emitted from the exhaust pipe. CO, NO_x and HC are the only gaseous pollutants that occur in significant quantities.

The result of growing travel demand is a multiplicity of transport systems ranging from non-motorised modes to the latest technology in cars and buses. Consequently, congestion, accidents and increasing levels of emissions from vehicles are contributing to the deteriorating environment. The situation in cities has reached a stage where the ambient air quality has perceivably deteriorated, establishing the need to take certain actions to control pollution levels. The Supreme Court of India passed orders directing local and state governments to take measures to minimise the air pollution generated from transport systems. Following orders of the court, the local government of Delhi implemented the following measures over a period of six years, i.e., from 1996 to 2002:

- Improved vehicular technology and stringent emission norms for vehicles.
- Fuel quality improvements.
- Phasing out of old vehicles.
- Introduction of cleaner fuel [namely compressed natural gas (CNG)].

Each of these measures was targeted separately for each of the sub-systems of transport. Understandably, each of these measures has contributed significantly to the reduction of air pollutants coming from vehicle exhausts.

Issues and Challenges Facing the Urban Road Transport Sector

The major challenges facing the sector are:

- Cities are growing in size and population.
- Increasing energy consumption.
- Increasing congestion.
- Local air and noise pollution is worsening.
- GHG emissions.
- Quality of life is deteriorating in general.

Transport is the second largest consumer of energy and the growth of transport leads to pressure on limited availability of non-renewable energy. A gradual shift in passenger and freight movement from rail to road-based transportation has also been observed over the years. Also, the fuel consumption by road transport sector in India has increased in the recent past. Petrol and diesel consumption has increased over the years, registering an annual average growth rate of 8.0 per cent and 7.2 per cent respectively. Fuel consumption by motor vehicles in India was approximately 1.0 per cent of the world fuel consumption by road transport sector during 1991. Transportation energy demand could grow even faster than anticipated if all of the new highway projects currently under consideration are completed. Diesel usage in India is expected to be much higher than gasoline. At present, road transport is the largest consumer of high-speed diesel (HSD) in the country, accounting for about 75 per cent of the total consumption. The consumption of the large quantity of fuel by the motor vehicles is mainly responsible for deteriorating air quality and ever-increasing pollution loads.

Air Pollution

Delhi is one of the most rapidly expanding mega cities as established above. Travel needs in Delhi are mainly met by road transport and the city has a total road length of about 30,000 km.

Travel demand has increased tremendously during the last three decades by more than two times in terms of per capita trip rate (vehicular) in a day from 0.45 in 1969 to about 1.0 in 2001. The major modes of transportation are buses, private vehicles (namely cars and two-wheelers), taxis, auto rickshaws and bicycles in the order of total trips made in a day. But the trips made by car and two-wheelers have increased significantly as compared to the year 2001, whereas bus trips have reduced and redistributed among the other modes such as Delhi Metro (a rapid rail transit system) and cycle rickshaws. Further, the average trip lengths have increased marginally for all modes of transport as per recent estimates. This increase in average trip lengths clearly demonstrates that the compact city concept has gradually diminished, resulting in longer trip lengths that are further aggravating the pressure on the existing road network and increase in vehicular emissions. Therefore, a proper assessment of pollution loads from vehicular traffic is an essential requisite to arrive at policy measures which can enable proposition of appropriate remedial measures to control the menace of air pollution.

This aspect is very aptly emphasised in the CRRI study (2002) on Urban Road Traffic and Air Pollution (URTRAP), which deals with the quantification of the travel demand and associated pollution loads in a scientific manner. In the URTRAP study, carried out jointly by CRRI (New Delhi), National Environmental Engineering Research Institute (Nagpur) and the Indian Institute of Petroleum (Dehradun) on behalf of the Mashelkar Committee and sponsored by the Ministry of Petroleum and Natural Gas (MoPNG), employing the vehicle-kilometres travelled (VKT) on the city roads, total pollution load has been estimated for each of the four pollutants, namely CO, NO_x, HC and PM in selected Indian cities (Table 6.1).

Again, in August 2008, the Society of Indian Automobile Manufactures (SIAM) entrusted CRRI with the task of estimating the quantum of travel demand in terms of VKT by each mode and of quantifying the associated pollution loads in Delhi. This 2009 report included estimation of traffic flows and related vehicular emissions generated based on VKT on the Delhi road network. The study results show that VKT has increased almost two times as compared to the 2002 CRRI study.

On the contrary, associated pollution loads have significantly reduced as compared to the 2002 CRRI study and the reduction is of the order of 37 per cent, 31 per cent, 25 per cent and 23 per cent

Table 6.1

Estimated Pollution Load in Selected Cities (2002)

City	*Pollution Load (in metric tonnes per day)*			
	Carbon Monoxide	*Nitrogen Oxide*	*Hydrocarbon*	*Particulate Matter*
Delhi	421.84	110.45	184.37	12.77
Mumbai	189.55	46.37	89.93	10.58
Kolkata	137.50	54.09	47.63	10.80
Chennai	177.00	27.30	95.64	7.29
Bengaluru	207.04	29.72	117.37	8.11
Hyderabad	163.95	36.89	90.09	8.00
Kanpur	28.73	7.25	11.70	1.91
Agra	24.93	5.99	12.23	1.41

Source: Central Road Research Institute, 2002.

Figure 6.3

Comparison of Pollution Loads in Delhi in 2002 and 2009

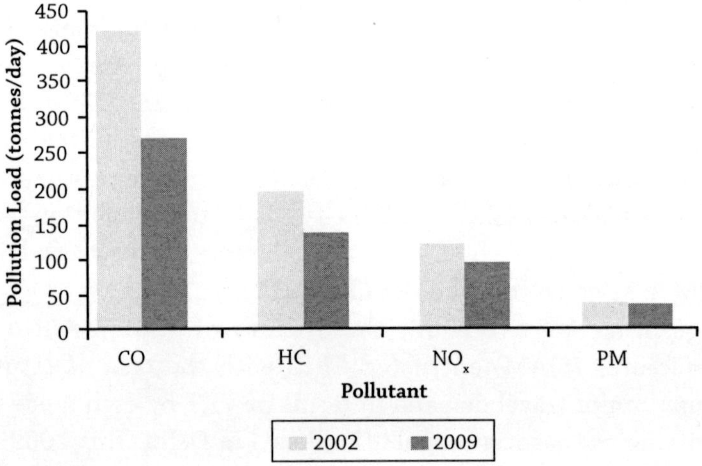

Source: Central Road Research Institute, 2009.

in CO, HC, NO_x and PM respectively (Figure 6.3). This reduction in pollution loads can be attributed to: the age profile of vehicles operating with improved technologies such as BS-I, BS-II and BS-III; full-scale implementation of CNG as a fuel in autos, taxis and buses; increased proportion of CNG-run private cars; and other factors such as four-stroke engines in two-wheelers and improvements in fuel quality. It is to be noted here that the above-mentioned pollution loads were calculated assuming the existence of typical Indian driving cycle (IDC) on Delhi roads by considering the Central Pollution Control Board (CPCB) emission factors.

Impact of Congestion on Emissions

Indian roads are congested and are of poor quality. Lane capacity is low—most national highways are two lanes or less. A quarter of all India's highways are congested, reducing truck and bus speeds to 30-40 km per hour. Road maintenance remains significantly underfunded—only around one-third of maintenance needs are met. This leads to the deterioration of roads as well as high transport costs for users. Urban centres are also severely congested. The dramatic growth in vehicle ownership—at about 15 per cent a year during the past decade—has reduced rush hour speeds to 5-10 km per hour in the central areas of major cities.

However, since traffic congestion is so acute for most part of the day on major arterials and sub-arterials of the city, the effect of congestion on Delhi road network was appropriately accounted for and associated pollution loads were also determined separately in the above-mentioned study by CRRI in 2009. The study output emphasises the impact of policy interventions in reducing pollution loads considerably. However, the absence of appropriate travel demand management measures for tackling the increased travel demand has resulted in causing frequent bottlenecks at most of the mid-blocks, intersections and at the mouth of the flyovers on Delhi road network, which has nullified the gains achieved from improved vehicle technology and fuel quality improvements.

Employing the VKT on the city roads, total pollution loads have been estimated for each of the four pollutants. The estimated daily pollution loads of CO, HC, NO_x and PM from vehicles are observed in tonnes per day to be 264.55, 127.54, 82.53 and 9.81 respectively in 2009 (Figure 6.4). As already stated, these pollution loads have significantly reduced since 2002. Subsequently, the pollution loads were estimated by increasing the loads by cars and buses with separate factor given they are more affected than compared to two-wheelers and autos. Goods vehicles are less affected as they travel mostly during night hours. The estimated pollution loads of CO, HC, NO_x and PM with congestion effect is around 391.5, 181.9, 126.2 and 14.1 tonnes per day respectively.

Figure 6.4

Comparison of Pollution Loads in Delhi with Congestion Effect

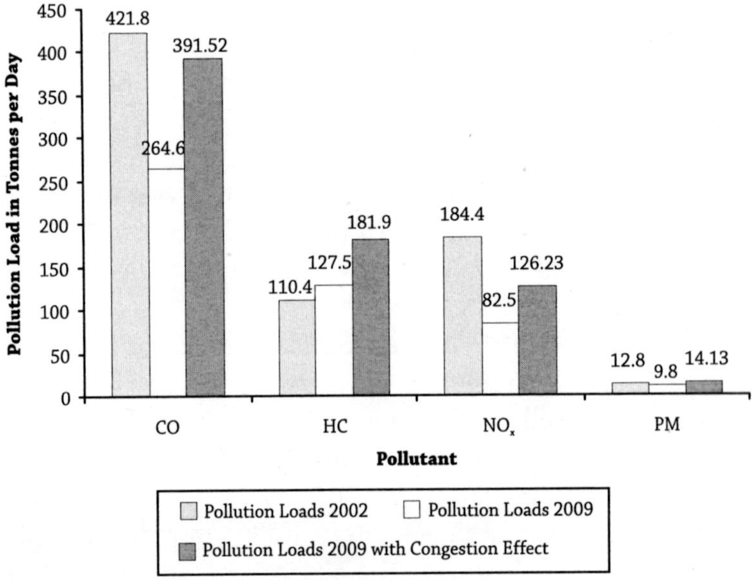

Source: Central Road Research Institute, 2009.

Health Impacts of Air Pollution

Private passenger vehicles are in high demand in urban areas and car ownership is growing rapidly at over 10 per cent per annum. A drastic increase in the number of two-wheelers has also been observed, increasing from 8 per cent in 1951 to 70.9 per cent in 2003. On the other hand, the share of public transport has severely declined, particularly the share of buses, which declined from 11 per cent to 1.1 per cent during the same period.

Vehicles have been found to emit large quantities of CO, HCs, NO_x and other toxic substances including fine particles. Emissions from old and in-use private vehicles with old technology (e.g., two- and three-wheelers with two-stroke engines) are very high. Impact of the quality of fuel and the level of vehicle technology on the quality of the air can be easily observed.

Vehicular source emissions are extremely complex and comprise hundreds of compounds that are present in the atmosphere as gases, aerosols and particulates. Many of these compounds are transformed in the atmosphere to generate secondary pollutants, i.e., photochemical smog, acid aerosols and carcinogenic HCs that are sometimes more harmful than their precursors emitted directly (Table 6.2). Some of these compounds such as various species of volatile organic compounds (VOCs) are highly reactive in nature. They, along

Table 6.2

Source of Emissions in Vehicles and Their Health Effects

Pollutant	*Health Effects*
CO	A product of incomplete combustion. Interferes with the absorption of oxygen by red blood cells and can affect the nervous system.
HC	A product of incomplete combustion and evaporating from fuel. Symptoms akin to those during drunkenness as well as eye irritation, coughing, sneezing and drowsiness. Can cause cancer and other diseases. An input to photochemical smog.
NO_X	Product of reaction between atmospheric N_2 and O_2 at high temperature conditions similar to vehicle engines. Decreases gaseous exchange in the blood thus reducing lung function values. A precursor pollutant to photochemical smog formation.
SO_2	Product of oxidation of sulphur present in the fuel. Constriction of air passages in respiratory tract. An input to smog and acid rain.
Particulates	Mainly emitted from diesel as smoke, from wear and tear of tyres and brake linings. Can deeply penetrate into the respiratory system, irritating lung tissues and can cause long-term disorders, are toxic and lead to greater infant mortality and anaemia in general.
Benzo-pyrene	By-product of incomplete combustion of diesel. Potentially mutagenic and carcinogenic.
Benzene	Constituent of gasoline and vehicle exhausts. Carcinogenic and can cause leukaemia.
CO_2	GHG emitted in the largest quantity by vehicles. Paradoxically, CO_2 is a product of good combustion and not bad.

Source: Adapted from USEPA, Integrated Risk Information System, 2007; and N. Perez-Padilla, R., *The Health Effects of Indoor Air Pollution Exposure in Developing Counties*. WHO, Report No. WHO/SDE/OEH/02.05.2002.

with NO_x, are mainly responsible for the formation of photochemical oxidants. Besides these, motor vehicles are also a major source of a number of toxic air pollutants; many of the individual VOC species including benzene, 1-3 butadiene, formaldehyde, acetaldehyde, polycyclic aromatic hydrocarbons (PAHs) are considered to be carcinogenic in nature.

With the impending hazards of global warming, climate change, ozone-layer depletion, coupled with the growing risks of not only chronic respiratory problems but dreaded terminal diseases including cancer, all within its wide repertory, the fast degrading air quality has become the most critical global environmental concern. Rapidly growing populations, changing consumption-oriented life-styles, rather poor infrastructural facilities, and lax urban planning and implementation have only worsened the malady in Indian cities. Fine particulates, volatile organics, oxides of nitrogen, ozone, heavy metals, etc., are hazardous; extremely harmful air-pollutants are in high concentrations in urban pockets and/or have shown rising trends. Strategies must be devised to fight against these health hazards.

Air Quality Management

Urban air quality management has become a very complex issue, particularly in developing countries. It is also for the reason that the knowledge related to this subject has evolved over the years wherein the conventional methods have failed to achieve the desired results. Some suggestions for air quality management are given below and in Table 6.3:

- Science-based air pollution management has been the need of the hour, where the monitoring is linked with emission inventory and both of these are used for modelling to arrive at the current and future scenario.
- Advanced tools of air quality dispersion, receptor modelling, inventorisation, health-based standards development, etc., are being used in many countries. The advancement is very rapid and therefore there is a need to review the current status of air quality management. The tools and

Table 6.3

Typical Measures for Abatement of Air Pollution from Motor Vehicles

Type of Measure	*Command and Control Measures*	*Market-based Incentives*	*Additional Measures*
Vehicle targeted	Emission standards and related measures for new vehicles • Emission standards • Certification • Assembly line testing • Recall • Warranty Emission standards and inspection programmes for in-use vehicles • Emission standards • I/M programmes • Roadside inspection programmes Emission restrictions on imported vehicles	• Vehicle emission fees • Differential vehicle registration fees and taxes • Vehicle retrofit programmes • Vehicle replacement or scrappage incentives	
Fuel targeted	Gasoline standards • Lead • Volatility • Benzene and other aromatics • Reformulated gasoline • Oxygenated gasoline Diesel fuel standards • Sulphur • Cetane number • Aromatics and density Alternative fuels • Compressed natural gas • Liquefied petroleum gas • Methanol • Ethanol	• Fuel taxes • Tradable permits and credits	
Transport management	• Driving bans • On-street parking and trading restrictions • Traffic priority measures for buses • Ride sharing • Staggered work hours • Speed limits • Land use planning	• Road pricing • Area licensing • Staggered work hours • Speed limits • Land use planning	• Provision of public transport services • Promotion of non-motorised transport • Provision of off-street parking

Source: Based on Carbajo and Faiz, 1994.

techniques being used and developed internationally need to be internalised for further developments which are India specific for high relevance and impact.

- The application and revision of scientific understanding as well as management of such problems need immediate adoption.
- The growth of economy is likely to experience major barriers from the environment sector in coming years. Some of the urban centres have already seen a decline where the businesses are looking at urban air quality as a major factor which could negatively impact them and their workers. There is a need for an integrated approach to transport, energy and environment so as to foster the development of various transport modes in a manner that will lead to the realisation of an efficient, sustainable, safe and regionally balanced transportation system, and to promote a sustainable transport system with increased emphasis on safety, energy efficiency, environment conservation and social impact.
- There is a need for a holistic and coordinated approach towards consideration of transport and environmental implications.
- There is a need for substituting personalised road transport with public transportation modes and rail transport, improving efficiency and promoting alternate fuels (CNG, biofuels, electric vehicles).
- A more prudent move to achieve a sustainable future would be to reduce the volume of travel demand itself by specifying the ways and means to reduce VKT with a new roadmap focusing on appropriate travel demand management (TDM) measures/polices in order to relieve congestion on road network. Furthermore, integration of TDM measures in urban transport policy can help in reducing pollution levels in Delhi. This involves adapting more environmentally friendly and sustainable lifestyles, such as using vehicles only for very important needs, avoiding luxury travels and choosing the most energy-efficient options.

- Environment and energy issues need to be addressed as integral parts of transport planning and implementation rather than as isolated studies. A future vision should focus on achieving long-term environmental, energy, social and economic sustainability.

References

Carbajo, José and Asif Faiz (1994). "Motor Vehicle Emissions Control: Some Policy Options for Developing Countries", *Science of the Total Environment* 146–147: 11-18, May 23.

Central Road Research Institute (2009). *Urban Road Traffic and Air Pollution in Delhi (URTRAP).* Final Report Submitted to Society of Indian Automobile Manufactures (SIAM). New Delhi. India.

————. (2002). *Urban Road Traffic and Air Pollution (URTRAP).* Report Submitted to Ministry of Petroleum and Natural Gas, Government of India. New Delhi.

CPCB (2000a). "Air Quality Status and Trends in India", *National Ambient Air Quality Monitoring Series* NAAQMS/14/1999-2000. New Delhi: Central Pollution Control Board, Ministry of Environment and Forests, Government of India.

————. (2000b). *Transportation Fuel Quality for Year 2005.* PROBES/78/2000-01. New Delhi: Central Pollution Control Board, Ministry of Environment and Forests, Government of India.

————. *http//www.cpcb.nic.in*

Helio International 3i Network (2001). *Energy and Sustainable Development in India: Sustainable Energy Watch 2005/06.*

Horowitz, J.L. (1982). *Air Quality Analysis for Urban Transportation Planning*. Cambridge, Massachusetts: MIT.

Jalihal, S.A., K. Ravinder and T.S. Reddy (2005). "Traffic Characteristics of India", Proceedings of the *Eastern Asia Society for Transportation Studies (EASTS)* 5: 1009-24. Available from *http://www.easts.info/on-line/proceedings_05/1009.pdf*

Madhu, E., K. Ravinder and S. Velmurugan (2010). "Traffic Characteristics of Delhi", in *TRANSTEC 2010 International Conference Proceedings*. New Delhi. April 5-6.

Ministry of Road Transport and Highways (2007). *Road Transport Year Book 2004-05.* New Delhi: Transport Research Wing, Ministry of Shipping, Road Transport and Highways, Government of India.

OECD (1995). *Motor Vehicle Pollution: Reduction Strategies Beyond 2001.* France: Organization of Economic Cooperation and Development Publication Service.

OECD/IEA (2005). *Making Cars More Fuel Efficient: Technology for Real Improvements on the Road.* European Conference of Ministers of Transport (ECMT) and International Energy Agency (IEA).

Ravinder, K., E. Madhu and S. Gangopadhyay (2010). "Vehicular Emission Norms vs. Vehicular Pollution Loads in Delhi", in *TRANSTEC 2010 International Conference Proceedings*. New Delhi. April 5-6.

Rastogi, Anupam (ed.) (2006). *India Infrastructure Report: Urban Transport.* New Delhi: Oxford University Press.

Ravinder, Kayitha and E. Madhu (2010). "Impact of National Auto Fuel Policy Emission Norms on Vehicular Pollution Loads in Delhi", Paper published in the souvenir of the national get-together held at CRRI. New Delhi. March 5-6.

Sherwood, P.T. and P.H. Bowers (1970). *Air Pollution from Road Traffic: A Review of the Present Position.* Crowthorne, U.K.: Transport Road Research Laboratory, LR 352.

Shiva, V. (2004). "The Impact of Globalisation on India's Environment", *Global Ecology,* May 7.

Shukla, Anuradha and Masood Alam (2010). "Assessment of Real World On-Road Vehicle Emissions under Dynamic Urban Traffic Conditions in Delhi", *International Journal of Urban Sciences* 14(2).

7

PAWAN KUMAR

Pedestrian Planning in Urban Areas

Introduction

The sidewalk for pedestrians is an access and egress mode to any public transport system. It provides a crucial link among the modes in a journey chain. It is roughly estimated that public transport users walk at least four times every day. Therefore, better pedestrian infrastructure is required for easy and better accessibility to public transport. Today, multiple modes of public transport are available in Indian metropolitan cities, making public transport a multimodal public transport system which combines two or more modes to provide efficient, rapid and environmentally compatible movement. In this context, the role of walking is vital. Further, due to expansion of city boundaries and urban sprawls, the single mode of transport is neither viable nor efficient, as the spatial separation between commuters' residences and work places has increased. Consequently, integration of pedestrian with multimodal public transport enhances share of non-motorised modes and reduces use of personalised vehicles. Pedestrian planning is therefore considered an integral part of overall transport system.

The pedestrian infrastructure has major contribution in urban mobility, since a vast majority of people, particularly the urban poor who have no access to personalised mode or cannot afford public transport for daily commuting, are pedestrians. In fact, low-income households are captive pedestrians trying to reach the nearest bus stops, metro stations and workplaces. Similarly, pedestrian safety is a crucial issue, particularly for women, children, old-aged persons, disabled, etc. The use of non-motorised modes such as walking, bicycles and cycle rickshaws has become extremely risky, as these modes have to share the same right of way with motorised modes.

According to the National Crime Records Bureau of the Indian Ministry of Home Affairs, pedestrians accounted for 9.1 per cent share in road accident deaths during 2010 as compared to 8.8 per cent in 2009. Clearly, safety of the pedestrian is one of the challenges for architects, engineers, town planners, urban local bodies and policy makers to make movement safe on the roads. Safety is also an area of concern in planning and designing of pedestrian facilities.

Pedestrians in Urban Areas

The Indian Ministry of Urban Development formulated the National Urban Transport Policy in 2006 with the aim of ensuring safe, affordable, quick, comfortable, reliable and sustainable access for the growing number of city residents to jobs, education, recreation and other needs within cities. It encourages greater use of public transport and non-motorised modes by offering central financial assistance for this purpose. It also gives priority to: non-motorised transport including pedestrians; construction of safe pedestrian crossings at busy intersections and high traffic corridors; and formulation and implementation of specific 'area plans' in congested urban areas that propose exclusive zones for non-motorised transit.

The M/s Wilbur Smith Associates conducted transport surveys in 30 Indian cities in 2007 and submitted the report to the Ministry of Urban Development. The report states the share of pedestrians in various cities classified on the basis of population (Table 7.1). It illustrates the share of pedestrians vary from 22 per cent in a city with a population of more than 80 lakh to 34 per cent in a city with a population less than 5 lakh.

Further, Table 7.2 provides a clear picture of the share of pedestrians in various metropolitan cities. It reveals that Mumbai has the highest share of pedestrians (27%) as compared to Bengaluru (26%), Hyderabad (22%) and Delhi (20%). A comparative share of pedestrian, bicycle and intermediate para transit (IPT) in selected metropolitan cities is illustrated in Figure 7.1.

Table 7.1

Mode Share of Pedestrian (Walking) in Selected Indian Cities, 2007

S. No.	*Cities Classified According to Population*	*Per cent of Walking*
1.	Less than 5 lakh (plain terrain)	34
2.	Less than 5 lakh (hill terrain)	57
3.	5-10 lakh	32
4.	10-20 lakh	24
5.	20-40 lakh	25
6.	40-80 lakh	25
7.	More than 80 lakh	22

Source: Wilbur Smith Associates and Ministry of Urban Development, Government of India, New Delhi.

Table 7.2

Share of Pedestrians, Bicycles and Intermediate Para Transit in Selected Metropolitan Cities of India, 2007

(in %)

S. No.	*City*	*Walk*	*Bicycle*	*Intermediate Para Transit*
1.	Delhi	20	12	6
2.	Mumbai	27	6	7
3.	Kolkata	19	11	4
4.	Chennai	22	9	8
5.	Bengaluru	26	7	7
6.	Hyderabad	22	9	7

Source: Wilbur Smith Associates and Ministry of Urban Development, Government of India, New Delhi.

Moreover, walking distance is a function of 'pedestrian safety' if informal and shortest path is selected at trip origin, transfer point and metro station. In most of the cases, pedestrian safety is associated with pedestrian environment. The encroachment of footpaths adversely affects pedestrian safety and requires strict enforcement. Walkable areas in cities need proper planning so that commuters can walk to transit stations easily and comfortably at all times. The share of walking can be enhanced by developing local walking strategies for local transport activities.

Figure 7.1

Comparison of Share of Pedestrians in Selected Metropolitan Cities of India, 2007

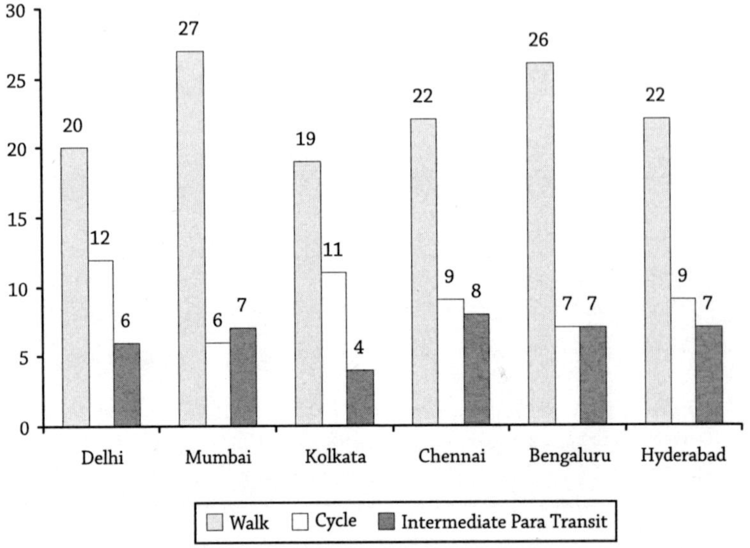

Source: Wilbur Smith Associates and Ministry of Urban Development, Government of India, New Delhi.

Basic Issues in Pedestrian Planning

The planning and design of pedestrian facilities is as systematic and scientific as highway design. It requires a multi-dimensional approach which covers the following basic issues:

- Man (M1): The human factors in terms of human body dimensions, locomotion characteristics, sight, vision, disability, etc., have direct influence in planning and design of pedestrian. Further, human behaviour, psychological preferences to understand space requirements, pedestrian traffic relationship, etc., are some of the important considerations.
- Machinery (M2): It includes use of various mechanical devices such as escalators, moving walks, pedestrian skywalks, elevated and underground pedestrian networks and their horizontal and vertical connectivity.

- Methods (M3): It includes sufficient right of way (ROW) width for the provision of pedestrian, bicycles, cycle rickshaws and multiuse zone. Similarly, walkable design, zoning regulations, movement pattern inside and outside transport terminals, stations, etc., are considered.
- Materials (M4): The use of appropriate materials, techniques, colors, texture, structural stability, maintenance, etc., is as important as the design itself.
- Money (M5): It includes funds and budget for repairs and maintenance of pedestrian facilities and infrastructure by the concerned authorities and urban local bodies. It requires sufficient budgetary allocation in annual plans.

Many Indian cities are naturally built for walking and cycling, and therefore, a majority of destinations in residential areas are accessible by non-motorised transport. Indian cities are characterised by high density and mixed land uses, which further provide captive advantages to pedestrians. Thus, pedestrian facilities should be properly designed in various land use zones. Table 7.3 describes a comprehensive design attribute related to pedestrian facilities.

Furthermore, it is essential to prioritise investments for non-motorised transport, particularly for pedestrian facilities. It provides impetus to a new approach which promotes the avoid-shift-improve approach to public transport.

Learning Experience

Network and Walkable Improvement Project, Nanded

The Network and Walkable Improvement Project under the central-government-funded Jawaharlal Nehru National Urban Renewal Mission (JNNURM) was conceived in 2006 in Nanded. Nanded is one of the mission cities situated in the state of Maharashtra. The city municipality and private firms took up this project. A major initiative to improve the streets of the city was undertaken. About 50 km of streets in Nanded were redesigned, improved and built. The pedestrian pathways have been planned in such a way that space is allotted to pedestrians, bicyclists and a

Table 7.3

Design Components of Pedestrian Facilities and Their Characteristics

S. No.	*Design Components*	*Characteristics*
1.	Attractiveness	It encompasses more than aesthetic design to attract more pedestrians to walk and enjoy the scenic beauty along transit corridors.
2.	Continuity	Continuity of pedestrian pathways/sidewalks is important for disabled and old age users. Continuous ups and downs make the sidewalk more uncomfortable.
3.	Convenience	Circuitous routings and grade discontinuities of pedestrian pathways cause inconvenience. These must be avoided.
4.	Coherence	An ideal pedestrian system must connect all major traffic generators with direct linkages in a coherent and easily identifiable configuration.
5.	Encroachment	Informal commercial activities along the sidewalk to cater to day-to-day needs. Extent of encroachment must not rise to a level that the sidewalk facilities become inaccessible to pedestrians.
6.	Footpath Surface	Smooth surface without any crack or bump for comfortable walking.
7.	Footpath Width	Sufficient width of the sidewalk available to the pedestrians during peak hours.
8.	Imageability	Imageability of pedestrian environment requires descriptive elements that comprise space, edges, paths, nodes and landmarks, which must be logically organised to clearly express the image of 'pedestrian space' as a liveable environment for better and pleasant mobility.
9.	Obstructions	Hoardings, garbage bins, electric poles, trees, letter box, telephone wire box, etc., cause obstructions and must be properly planned and placed.
10.	Potential for Vehicle Conflicts	Pedestrian can be protected from vehicle conflicts by raised footpaths and guardrails. Sidewalks need to be segregated from fast moving vehicles on the roads.

Source: Information obtained by the author from various sources.

multiuse zone that includes parking space, bus stops and hawker platforms in a way that they do not encroach upon the footpaths or roads. Pedestrian crossings, pedestrian refuge islands, signage and traffic signals have been provided. Intersections have also been designed and cobbled. Even the entry and exit of adjacent buildings were changed to make these more pedestrian friendly, giving a taste of new urbanism.

Fazilka Town as a Pedestrian City

Fazilka town is one of the best examples in the country of a pedestrian city. It is situated in Firozpur district of Punjab on the India-Pakistan border. The town has a population of about 68,000 and the number of vehicles is 45,000. On 21 November 2009, it was decided to remove one source of congestion on the roads, i.e., no entry of cars. Fazilka created 'car-free Zone' at Ghanta Ghar Market from 10 am to 7 pm. The vendors in the area are happy because their sales have soared. Customers are more relaxed, as they do not have to jostle with parked vehicles. Furthermore, the cycle rickshaw eco-cabs[1] were established and Fazilka has perhaps become the first town in India which has a dial-a-rickshaw facility.

Bandra (East)-Kala Nagar Skywalk, Mumbai

Skywalk is an elevated walkway dedicated to pedestrians connecting the railway stations/high concentration commercial areas to less congested areas as destination points. Mumbai Metropolitan Region Development Authority (MMRDA) has initiated a project of skywalks under the Station Area Traffic Improvement Scheme (SATIS). It integrates pedestrian movement with railway stations. The important features of Bandra (East) Kala Nagar Skywalk are as follows:

- Length of the Skywalk : 1,300 metres
- Width of the Skywalk : 4.0 metres clear walkway
- Structural details : Elevated walkway of 4.0 metres X 3.0 metres framed structure with polycarbonate sheet as roofing and resting on 1.0 metre-diameter pier of height approximately 6.0 metres above the ground level

1. Eco-cabs are a telephonic cycle rickshaw service made available at doorstep through the network of call centres, similar to dial-a-cab/taxi service. It was introduced in order to bridge the gap between demand and supply need of para transit mode as a public transport using the latest transportation management and technological tools (*www.ecocabs.org*).

- Number of staircases : Four
- Staircase location : Anant Kanekar Marg Police Chowki, near ONGC Building, Kala Nagar on either side of Sion-Dharavi Road
- Peak hour capacity : 5,500 commuters
- Opened to public : 24 June 2008

The Way Forward

The following areas of concern related to pedestrian planning have been identified for further course of action. Such actions can include short-term and long-term planning measures based on both local conditions and international perspectives.

Walking in hot, humid climate and high temperature is neither desirable nor comfortable in India. Commuters do not prefer to walk in both extreme summer and winter conditions. Therefore, it is important to design pedestrian facilities by using micro-climatic concept. Additionally, the brunt of extreme climatic conditions can be changed by using multimodal-oriented design in planning of pedestrian facilities. The concept of multimodal-oriented design encourages a mix of mobility options with diversion of land use planning and site design. It does not give preference to any one particular mode but creates a balance between various modes so that they may work to complement each other. It requires developing a balance and successful multimodal access plan; their efficient operations; strategies to achieve better integration of modes through physical design; commercial exploitation of the space available near bus stops/metro stations, etc.

Recently, various state governments have been developing IT/ BPO (information technology/business process outsourcing) towns, satellite towns, special economic zones (SEZs), etc. It is desirable that in the development of such townships, there must be provision for both pedestrian and bicycle tracks to reduce personalised motorised modes. However, if it is not possible to provide dedicated paths for pedestrians and cyclists, traffic-calming measures must be adopted to limit the speed of motorised vehicles for safe movement of pedestrians. Similarly, flyovers must be designed and constructed keeping in mind the movement needs of pedestrians.

As per the Bangkok 2020 Declaration: Sustainable Transport Goals for 2010-2020, it is the need of the hour to incorporate non-motorised components, particularly pedestrian components, in transport master plans and prioritise transport infrastructure investments to non-motorised transport. Similarly, the provisions for Nationally Appropriate Mitigation Actions (NAMAs) for Sustainable Transport should be adopted as per requirements. In the Indian context, the Comprehensive Mobility Plan (CMP) is prepared along with City Development Plan (CDP) to obtain financial assistance under JNNURM. If the same is focused on Environmentally Sustainable Transport (EST) strategies and targeting greenhouse gas (GHG) reduction, then it may help to achieve the objectives of sustainable transport under NAMA. A better planning and design of pedestrian facilities at initial stage may support sustainable growth of new towns and cities.

It is imperative today that urban local bodies come forward to develop infrastructure projects in small- and medium-sized towns. Sufficient budget has been allocated for road construction in many states, but it is important that road design must attach primacy to pedestrians and public transport. Therefore, public transport plans should be linked with pedestrian plans for better connectivity and mobility of commuters. It is also important that approval of all road projects should make adherence to pedestrian guidelines mandatory.

Pedestrian access to multimodal public transport requires supportive infrastructure and user friendly environment, which are not sufficient in present conditions due to many entrenched transport planning practices that are inherently auto centric. As a result, it is essential to recognise the importance of planning for people, not only for cars, and of planning for all kinds of people, not only the typical motorised vehicle users. It is critical to understand that 'Pedestrian Transit System' is an integral part of the public transport system and journey chain. Pedestrian facilities are relatively less costly and may be considered as a separate project on priority basis in public interest. Such projects could be a part of other projects such as station improvement scheme, terminal improvement, bus stand renovation project and traffic management packages.

References

Fruin, John J. (1979). "Pedestrian Transportation", in G.E. Gray and L.A. Hoel (eds.), *Public Transportation: Planning, Operations and Management*. New Jersey: Prentice Hall Inc.

Government of India (2005). *Jawaharlal Nehru National Urban Renewal Mission Guidelines*. New Delhi: Ministry of Urban Development.

———. (2006). *National Urban Transport Policy*. New Delhi: Ministry of Urban Development.

Kumar, P. *et al.* (2009a). "Design Approach for Multi Modal Transport System", *Architecture: Time, Space and People* 9(12): 26-33, December.

———. (2009b). "Multi Modal Transportation System in Urban India: A Way Forward towards Seamless Transport", *Civil Engineering Journal* 90: 13-18, November. Institution of Engineers (India).

———. (2010). "Pedestrian Access to Multi Modal Public Transport", *Indian Journal of Transport Management:* 4-16, January-March. Pune.

Mhaisekar, Deepak (2009). *Presentation on JNNURM Works in Nanded*. November. Nanded: Nanded Waghala City Municipal Corporation.

Mumbai Metropolitan Region Development Authority (2008). *Mumbai Urban Transport Project (Skywalk: Improved Travel Comfort for Mumbai Cars)*. Mumbai.

Ryan, Sherry and Lawrence F. Frank (2009). "Pedestrian Environments and Transit Ridership", *Journal of Public Transportation* 12(11): 39-48.

8

ROHIT CHATURVEDI

Inland Waterways: Transport Solution for Indian Cities

The Case of Mumbai

Introduction

Water bodies included in the definition of waterways comprise canals, lakes, rivers, water courses, inlets and bays that are nearest to the shores of a nation and subject to its complete sovereignty.

India is endowed with 14,500 km of navigable inland waterways and a long coastline of around 7,500 km. Out of this, 5,000 km is navigable by large barges, and only 2,000 km is utilised and managed by the Inland Waterways Authority of India (IWAI), which was established in 1986.

There are five declared national inland waterways in India. In addition, declaration of commencement of a new waterway on the Barak River in the north-eastern part of India is under consideration. Waterways other than the national waterways fall under the jurisdiction of the respective states.

The length of the inland waterways is more than 20 per cent of the length of the railway network in India. However, the total traffic, passenger or freight, handled by the waterways is negligible, with the notable exception of the Mandovi River in Goa. The contrast is starker if compared with the national highways (NHs). The NHs constitute about 66,590 km and cater to nearly 40 per cent of the total road traffic. The major activities involving waterways are still centred around fishing and short-distance movement of passenger boats in very limited geographies.

There are arguments that most of the waterways are non-navigable and converting them to a navigable mode of transport is not feasible. It may be true that on a standalone basis, many of these projects may be not be financially feasible. However, when economic and environmental impacts are taken into account, a number of projects based on inland waterways are likely to emerge as viable. This applies to most of the infrastructure projects. A case in point is the Delhi Metro project, which is envisaged to cover full operations and maintenance (O&M) costs and is not likely to cover its capital cost.

Another fact worth noting is that only about half of the NH projects are planned to be developed through the build-operate-transfer (BOT) route. Further, many of the envisaged BOT projects will require grants. In essence, even the supposedly viable road projects require a substantial amount of funding from the government and are not feasible from a purely financial perspective.

The concept of inland waterways as an alternative transport system scores over its counterparts in many aspects such as less fuel consumption, less dependence on land and protection of water bodies.

In the above context, it is worthwhile to explore the option of inland waterways as an alternative to the existing transport system and as a supplement to the multimodal transport model. With the right model of development, many locations in India may emerge as candidates for the development of inland waterways for both passenger and freight movement. However, while a slew of initiatives have recently been taken[1] to transport goods like coal and fertilisers through inland waterways, enthusiasm to develop them as an alternative to urban transport systems is sorely lacking.

This paper highlights the possibility of designing an appropriate network of waterways in cities to supplement other modes of transport, particularly roads, in order to share traffic. The article also spotlights possible problems that will have to be overcome for the successful implementation of waterways.

1. Goa has been utilising Mandovi River to transport iron ore for quite some time.

Institutional, Regulatory, Legal and Tax Framework

Waterways in India can be divided into two categories, namely:

- National waterways.
- Other waterways.

The national waterways fall under the purview of IWAI, which came into existence after the enactment of the IWAI Act, 1985. The major highlight of this Act is that it empowers IWAI to permit construction of infrastructural facilities on the national waterways. Further, IWAI has been empowered to levy fees and charges for services or benefits rendered in relation to the use of the national waterways. All policy matters relating to the national waterways are dealt with by the Ministry of Shipping, in consultation with IWAI.

All the other waterways come under the jurisdiction of their respective state governments. The inland waterways in the states of Maharashtra, Gujarat and Tamil Nadu are under the control of respective maritime boards.

Another piece of legislation, the Inland Vessel (IV) Act, 1917, empowers the state governments to frame rules regarding the survey and registration of inland mechanically propelled vessels. Any Indian national can own and operate such vessels anywhere in the country if the vessel is registered under the IV Act, akin to the national permit for inland vessels.

Foreign direct investment (FDI) of up to 100 per cent that is allowed for infrastructure is applicable to inland water transport (IWT) infrastructure as well. Some of the benefits extended to the inland waterways sector are as follows:

- Concessions under Sections 33 and 33 AC of the IT Act, 1986, to be applicable to inland vessels as they are applicable to sea-going ships.
- Rate of depreciation of 25 per cent applicable for inland vessels at par with sea-going ships.
- Concessions under Section 80 IA-12 (CA) of the IT Act, 1996, available for investment in IWT infrastructure.

- Permission for duty-free import of plants, equipment and machineries for the development of inland waterways (certification to be provided by IWAI).

Thus, comprehensive institutional, fiscal and regulatory frameworks are in place to support inland waterway transport in India. However, there is a clear need to further strengthen the nodal body, i.e., IWAI, for implementing the initiative in terms of capacity building and increasing management bandwidth. Moreover, there are certain grey areas regarding the compatibility of regulatory aspects pertaining to IWT with other regulations such as the Customs Act. In addition, there is a strong need for empowering IWAI to increase coordination between the state authorities and various other stakeholders to successfully implement many projects, which requires the network approach rather than the corridor approach.

This is particularly important for projects related to the urban transport system, which require assistance from various agencies. The subsequent paragraphs underscore this fact with the help of a case study of the Mumbai Metropolitan Region, one of the most significant commercial centres of the country and endowed with a number of waterways.

Mumbai: A Model Case for Alternative Mode of Transport

In this article, an attempt has been made to drive home the point that even if inland waterways may not solve all the woes related to congestion arising out of vehicular traffic in Mumbai, considering inland waterways as an additional mode of transport may help in putting in place the 'networked connectivity' approach for an integrated multimodal transport system. The major problem in transport planning in India arises out of adopting the corridor approach rather than the network approach. In the corridor approach, the objective is to tackle the problem from one point to another. This approach is flawed, since in many cases, it means shifting a bottleneck from one place to another. Usually, scant regard is given to the fact that traffic in any corridor is fed by other tertiary movements and mode of transport.

Case in point is the freight traffic that is currently plying on Mumbai's roads that can be shifted to an alternative mode of transport, i.e., inland waterways. In order to understand this possibility, it is important to understand the geographical contours of the city and identify the areas where a solution using water bodies can be implemented.

Here, the Mumbai Metropolitan Region (MMR) has been taken as defined by the Mumbai Metropolitan Region Development Authority (MMRDA) Act, 1974. It includes the following districts:

- Mumbai city.
- Mumbai suburban district.
- Part of Thane district comprising:
    a. Thane, Kalyan, Bhiwandi, Ulhasnagar *tehsils,* and
    b. Part of Vasai *tehsil.*
- Part of Raigad district comprising:
    a. Uran *tehsil.*
    b. Part of Panvel, Karjat, Khalapur, Pen and Alibag *tehsils.*

Vehicular traffic in MMR is increasing at an alarming pace. According to studies conducted by the MMRDA Transport and Communications Division, the total population of personal, commercial and public vehicles in MMR was pegged at approximately 3.5 million in March 2008, with cars comprising over one-fourth of the total vehicle population. This number is growing at a significant pace of 12 per cent per annum. At this rate, the vehicular count will double in MMR in the next six to seven years, further aggravating the problem of traffic congestion.

A significant number of commercial vehicles exit or enter MMR. This is because MMR has two major ports within its limits, the Mumbai Port Trust (MbPT) and the Jawaharlal Nehru Port Trust. The latter is the largest container port in India. MbPT is located in the heart of the city's commercial centre, and any road traffic directed towards the port inevitably leads to the congestion of the road network.

MMR is connected to other principal cargo centres through the four main NHs. Mumbai is connected with the northern hinterland via NH-8 which connects MMR to Delhi and Ahmedabad. NH-4 and NH-17 connect Mumbai to Pune and other southern states respectively. NH-17 runs along the coast on the south of Mumbai. Cargo centres in central India are joined to MMR through NH-3.

The main entry points to MMR are Vasai, Dahisar Check Naka, Thane Check Naka and Vashi Check Naka.

Some of the illustrative routes for freight traffic with distance comparison under road and IWT mode are depicted in Table 8.1.

Table 8.1

Freight Traffic Routes and Distances by Road and IWT

Route	*Distance (in km)*	
	Road	*IWT*
Mumbai Port Trust–Bassein	40	54
Mumbai Port Trust–Thane	35	36
Mumbai Port Trust–Vashi	27	22
Mumbai Port Trust–Belapur	38	23
Mumbai Port Trust–Nagothane	97	57

Source: IWAI.

If freight traffic from the above locations can be shifted to IWT, there is a strong possibility of reducing the burden on the road network. In addition, the freight traffic plying on the inland waterways will not be subject to the various restrictions that are imposed on road movements. For example, commercial vehicles are not allowed to ply on roads in the city at certain times.

Advantages of IWT in Mumbai

It may be noted that shifting of traffic to IWT is likely to provide many other benefits in addition to decongesting the road network. Some of the benefits are enumerated as follows:

- Fuel saving: Fuel consumption by IWT is one-third of that entailed in travel by roads, for similar distances. Moreover, IWT is less prone to traffic jams that result in higher fuel consumption on road movements. Therefore, shifting to IWT is expected to result in significant fuel savings.

- Reduced carbon emission and pollution: As a corollary of the above, lesser fuel consumption will generate lesser carbon and other greenhouse gases (GHGs). Thus, adoption of the IWT mode will help in lessening environmental pollution. The IWT mode may also lessen sound pollution caused by vehicles.
- Decrease in number of accidents: The possibility of accidents is lower in IWT since vessels have to cross fewer intersections on their course. In addition, the commercial vehicles which use IWT will move out of road traffic.
- Direct and indirect employment: The development of IWT has similar benefits as the development of other infrastructure. Direct benefits are likely to arise out of construction and operations of land and marine infrastructure such as jetties, connecting roads, buildings, vessel O&M. Moreover, Indian shipbuilding may also get an upside from a large number of customised vessels which are required for moving vehicles, cargo and passengers. Indirect employment may get a fillip from ancillary services required for running the IWT services.
- Tourism potential: The possibility of inland waterways-based tourism such as cruises could also be explored, providing another incentive to develop inland waterways.
- Disaster back-up for bridge-connected parts: It may be noted that many parts of MMR are connected with bridges with no alternatives to match in terms of distance between the connected parts. IWT may provide additional connectivity in the case of a disaster and offer the required redundancy in the transport network.
- Increased vigilance: Increased activity on the waterways will spawn greater movement and reduce the chances of the waterways being used as conduit for unlawful activities.

Possible Challenges in Implementation

Despite the host of benefits IWT may offer to the city of Mumbai, there are significant challenges in implementing the transport system owing to myriad reasons. Some of the reasons are discussed in the ensuing paragraphs.

Design Considerations/Concerns

This is one of the most oft-repeated reasons employed by critics of IWT. The design concerns arise out of issues of navigability of the water channel and investment required to surmount the problems posed by technical difficulties.

Among other requirements, IWT needs a minimum draft to allow commercial vessels to ply. The minimum draft has to be available for round-the-year operations. This means that water channels should not only be dredged to obtain the required draft, but also maintained at that level. This particular requirement necessitates a recurring cost in the form of maintenance in addition to the one-time cost of capital dredging. The substantial cost involved in dredging to make a channel navigable acts as a major constraint for developing IWT.

In addition to the maintenance of depth, the width of a channel also restricts the type of vessels which could move in the channel. Another complexity in the case of Mumbai emanates from the fact that the waterways are interspersed by various overhead bridges, thus limiting the availability of air draft and the dimensions of vessels which could move into these channels. Other constraints with respect to land include last-mile connectivity and topography.

Although the technical constraints for IWT, as mentioned above, are stringent, the problem may be resolved through choosing a suitable vessel. The vessel would have appropriate design parameters in terms of draft,[2] beam[3]/LOA (length over all),[4] etc. with enough capacity to carry the traffic.

---

2. The distance between the bottom of the ship (the keel) to the level of water on the ships side (water line).
3. The maximum breadth of the ship, which is in the amidships (the area between forward and the aft portion) body.
4. Length over all (LOA): The length of a ship from the foremost point on the bow to the most aft point on the stern.

In sum, although the problems in the form of technical requirements may be challenging, these can be tackled with innovative measures such as customised design of vessels, and compatible land and marine side infrastructure.

Commercial Considerations/Concerns

Although seemingly intractable technical problems may be resolved through innovative mechanisms, these come with significant costs. This problem brings us to the commercial constraints that may be faced by IWT projects. Some of the problems and possible solutions are suggested below:

- Tariff-setting: Tariff-setting for IWT is an important determinant for the success of projects of this kind. If the tariffs are set too low, the project will become unviable and if they are fixed at a higher level, traffic will be difficult to attract. Such complexity makes tariff-setting a challenging proposition. A possible approach to set the tariffs may be to study segment-wise costs for different vehicles such as trucks and trailers to reach their destinations after entering the city. It may be noted that apart from the direct costs, commercial vehicles also have to wait to comply with city rules for plying in the city.
- Project structuring: Another challenge is structuring the project in such a way so as to make it attractive to investors. It should be emphasised that IWT will comprise the following two parts:
    - Jetty business.
    - Vessel business.

  Proper consideration needs to be given to setting tariffs and providing financial and other support to both sides of the project. The key factors which should be kept in mind are costs incurred by each segment of the project, and fiscal and tax support allowed for each segment.
- Double handling for freight cargo: It must be noted that double handling of cargo traffic is likely to render the project

unviable due to delays and extra handling cost. To address this problem, solutions like the introduction of the Ro-Ro vessel[5] may be considered.

- Cost of developing infrastructure: The cost of developing various elements could be reduced through holistic consideration of the technical constraints and design parameters for vessels and jetty infrastructure.

Administrative Issues

As discussed in the previous paragraphs, projects of this nature require coordination with multiple bodies. The smooth coordination and proper aligning of concerned authorities is a must for their successful implementation. In the case of Mumbai, the following bodies will have jurisdiction on some of the parts of the project: MbPT; Jawaharlal Nehru Port Trust; City and Industrial Development Corporation; Mumbai Metropolitan Region Development Authority; Maharashtra Maritime Board; municipal bodies (responsible for Octroi); and defense.

Regulatory Consideration/Concerns

In addition to the technical, administrative and commercial aspects, the IWT project may run into problems if compliance with a host of regulatory requirements is not observed. A few important regulations pertinent to IWT are: environmental regulations; The Coastal Regulation Zone Act; The Inland Vessel Act; and Rehabilitation and Resettlement Bill, 2011.

Conclusion

The above-mentioned case underscores the fact that in some urban agglomerations, IWT could be explored either as an alternative to an existing transport solution or as a supplementary mode. It

5. Roll-on/roll-off (RORO or ro-ro) ships are vessels designed to carry wheeled cargo, such as automobiles, trucks, semi-trailer trucks, trailers and railroad cars, that are driven on and off the ship on their own wheels. This is in contrast to lo-lo (lift-on/lift-off) vessels which use a crane to load and unload cargo (Wikipedia).

must also be borne in mind that different solutions may exist, as in the case of Mumbai, where freight traffic could be shifted to IWT with the proper designing and structuring of IWT projects, from institutional, technical and commercial points of view.

9

KAUSHIK RANJAN BANDYOPADHYAY

Towards Sustainable Low-Carbon Urban Mobility in India

Addressing the Concerns

Introduction

Transport plays a crucial role in development and constitutes a significant share of world energy consumption. Transportation primarily relies on petroleum which supplies nearly 95 per cent of the total energy used by the world transport and also accounts for nearly 60 per cent of all oil consumption. The transport sector has thus also been largely responsible for the pollution and greenhouse gas (GHG) emissions which pervade the planet (Kahn *et al.*, 2007).

As of 2005, the total final consumption of petroleum products for the world stands at 3,420 million tonnes of oil equivalent, of which 2,067 million tonnes or 60.4 per cent is consumed by the transport sector (Table 9.1). Table 9.1 further delineates that within the transport sector, road transport consumes the largest share of 76.0 per cent (1,571 million tonnes of oil equivalent).

Of the GHG emissions from transport sector, carbon dioxide (CO_2) comprises the lion's share.[1] As of 2005, total emission of CO_2 from the transport sector amounts to around 23 per cent of the world's energy-related CO_2 emissions (Figure 9.1). What is all the more worrying is that among all the end-use sectors, the growth of transport-related CO_2 emissions has been the highest over the past three decades (Figure 9.2).

1. Other GHGs include methane (CH_4), nitrous oxide (N_2O), hydrofluorocarbons (HFCs), perfluorocarbons (PFCs), and sulphur hexafluoride (SF6).

Table 9.1

World Petroleum Products Consumption by the Transport Sector, 2005

Sector	*Million Tonnes of Oil Equivalent*	*Percentage*
Road	1571	76
World marine bunkers	171	8.3
International aviation	140	6.8
Domestic aviation	106	5.1
Domestic navigation	36	1.7
Rail	35	1.7
Pipeline transport	5	0.2
Others	3	0.1
Total transport	2067	100

Source: International Energy Agency (IEA), 2007b.

Figure 9.1

World CO_2 Emission by Sector, 2005

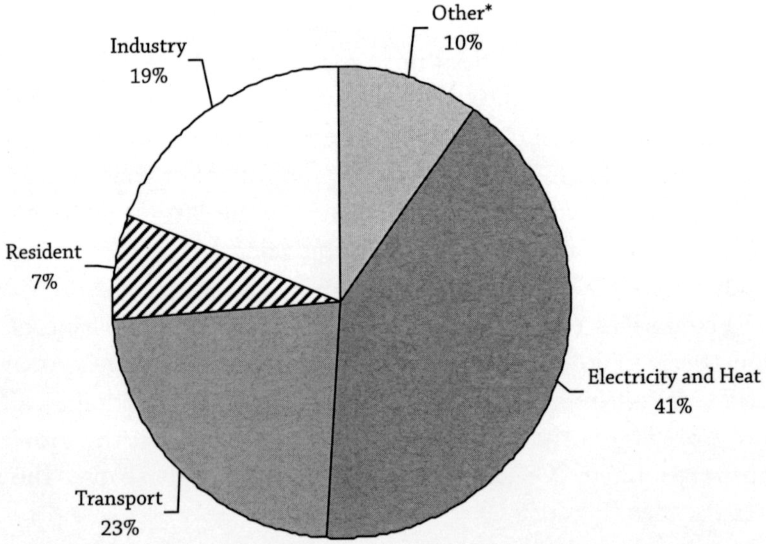

Note: *Other includes commercial/public services, agriculture, forestry, fishing, energy industries other than electricity and heat generation, and other emissions not specified elsewhere.

Source: IEA, 2007c.

Figure 9.2

CO_2 Emissions from Oil Combustion

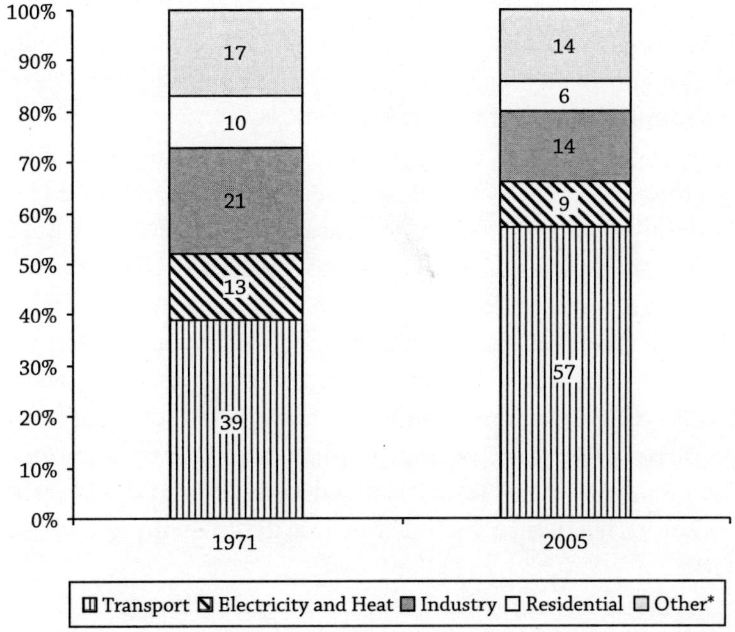

Note: *Other includes commercial/public services, agriculture, forestry, fishing, energy industries other than electricity and heat generation, and other emissions not specified elsewhere.

Source: IEA, 2007c.

Emerging Asian economies,[2] led by India and China, have been projected to account for much of the future growth in oil consumption and GHG emissions due to their strong economic growth trends and large populations. A more recent study on decomposition of CO2 emissions from transport sector in Asia carried out by Timilsina and Shrestha (2009) reveals that per capita GDP (income) and population growth accounts for the largest share of growth in CO_2 emissions in India and China.[3] According to projections made by

2. Includes Bangladesh, Bhutan, Cambodia, People's Republic of China (PRC), India, Indonesia, Lao PDR, Malaysia, Nepal, Pakistan, Philippines, Sri Lanka, Thailand and Vietnam.

3. The study took into consideration the annual time series data over the period 1980-2004.

Asian Development Bank (ADB), these two countries are expected to account for 45 per cent of the total world increase in oil use through 2025 (ADB, 2006). International Energy Agency (IEA) in their simulation exercise also indicates that the lion's share of the increase in oil demand from transport sector for the period 2006 to 2030 will come from India and China (IEA, 2008).

Figure 9.3 further disaggregates the transport CO_2 emissions across modes for 2005. The figure clearly shows that road transport has the largest contribution to emissions from fuel combustion in the transport sector and the on-road vehicles that are primarily responsible for such emissions are cars and light duty vehicles (LDVs), i.e., four-wheeled vehicles (including sports utility vehicles, small passenger vans with up to 8 seats) and trucks. Between 1990 and 2005, CO_2 emission from world transport sector rose by 37 per cent. During the same period, road transport emissions increased by 29 per cent in the industrialised countries and 61 per cent in other countries, which includes primarily developing nations (IEA, 2007d).

The Intergovernmental Panel on Climate Change (IPCC) advises in its fourth assessment report (AR4) that in order to avoid the worst impact of climate change, global CO_2 emissions must be cut by at least 50 per cent. Transport has a very significant role to play in realising this goal. Although all modes of transport would have to be a part of this emission cut, it is quite evident from the modal shares of CO_2 emissions (as shown in Figure 9.3) that the onus would fall primarily on road transport. In view of this, this paper focuses on challenges and opportunities of reducing energy consumption and CO_2 emissions from road transport in India.

Figure 9.3

Modal Shares of Transport CO_2 Emissions, 2005

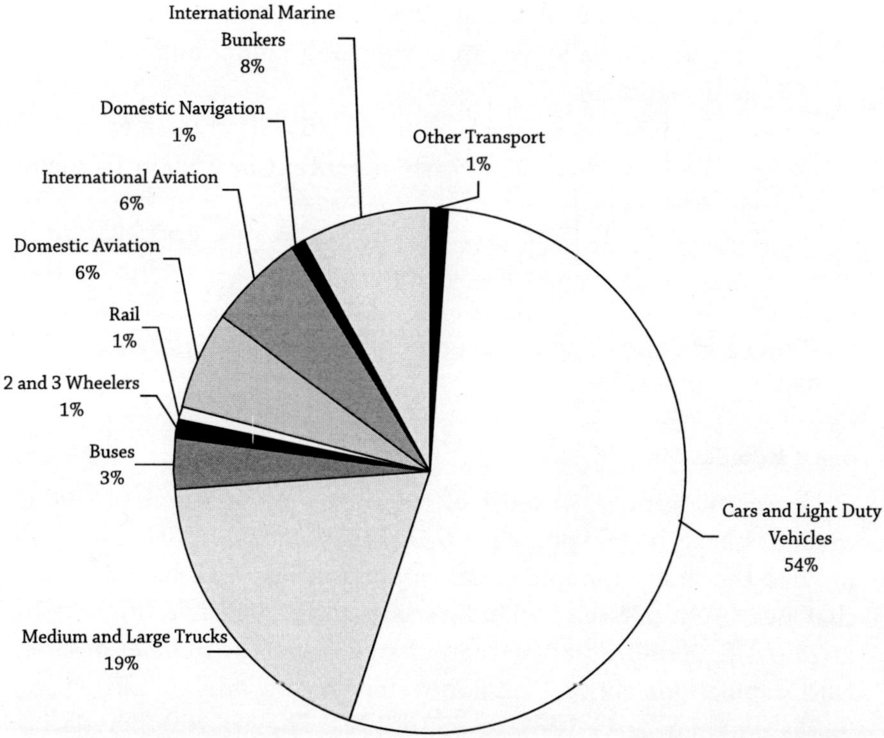

Source: IEA, 2007c.

Challenges in Reducing Energy Consumption and CO_2 Emissions from India's Urban Road Transport Sector

Within the transport sector in India, road transport has emerged as the dominant segment with a share of 4.5 per cent in India's GDP as of 2006-07. A lion's share of this road transport caters to urban metropolis. From 2000-01 to 2006-07, the annual average growth rate registered by GDP pertaining to the road transport sector was 9.4 per cent and was considerably higher than the overall growth rate of GDP during the same period which was around 6.9 per cent.[4] The

4. RBI, *Handbook of Statistics for the Indian Economy*, available at: *www.rbi.org.in*.

challenges in reducing CO_2 emissions and hence ensuring low-carbon road mobility in India could be clubbed under four broad categories:

- Challenges in controlling travel and freight activity (A).
- Structural challenges in influencing modal mix and hence modal shift (S).
- Challenges in reducing energy intensity (I) of modes.
- Challenges in reducing carbon content or carbon factor of the fuel (F) used.

This broad framework was first suggested by Schipper *et al.* (2000) and is usually referred to as ASIF framework.

Challenges in Controlling Travel and Freight Activity in Urban Transport in India (A)

Rapid Motorisation

Economic growth in most of the developing nations including India has been largely propelled by urban economic activities, which provide the bulk of employment opportunities. ADB has projected that nearly 38 per cent of India's population will live in cities by 2025 (ADB, 2006). Going by the Indian Census, the number of cities with populations above 1 million (referred to as million-plus cities) increased from 12 in 1981 to 35 in 2001. The growing population in urban areas led to de-densification of cities, with rapid growth in suburban areas. This trend of de-densification further led to increase in distances that are required to be travelled in order to access jobs and basic services, resulting in a rising demand for travel (Kahn *et al.*, 2007). The rising travel demand could hardly be served by the existing unsound, unattractive and inadequate public transport system which inevitably led to an increasing dependence on personalised vehicles.

Furthermore, post-liberalisation of the Indian economy, a number of new firms entered the automobile sector and came out with a large variety of cars in different segments (small, medium and large) and two-wheelers. The availability of a plethora of vehicles along with the easy financing of purchase at competitive interest rates increased the sale of private vehicles substantially during 1990s and afterwards. Way back in 2004-05, the number of cars sold in the country exceeded one million[5] and the number of two-wheelers exceeded six million. Figure 9.4 shows the vehicle fleet projections in India until 2025 as presented by ADB.

Figure 9.4

Projections of Vehicle Fleet

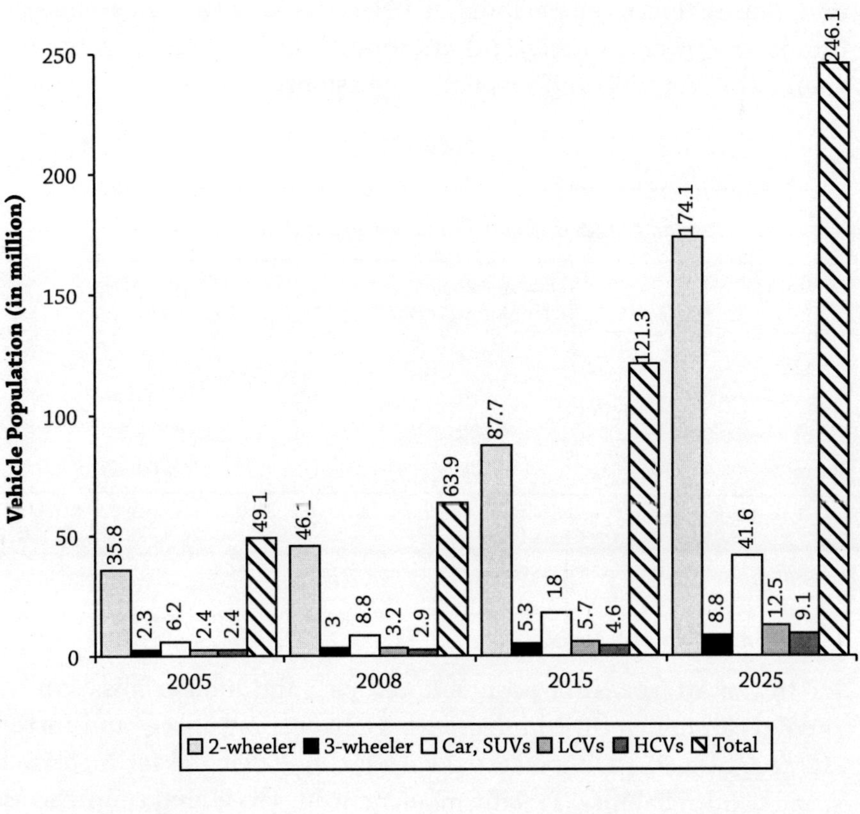

Source: ADB, 2006.

This is clearly a matter of serious concern. Although an on-road car consumes less energy and emits less CO_2 per vehicle km as compared to a high capacity public transport, the energy intensity

5. Available at: *http://www.siamindia.com/scripts/domestic-sales-trend.aspx*.

and CO_2 emission per passenger km for the former is much higher than that of the latter (as illustrated in Table 9.2).[6] As India shifts to a higher growth trajectory, the ownership of personal vehicles, particularly cars, will continue to grow at a rapid pace driven by rising per capita incomes and a growing trend of urbanisation coupled with growing aspirations of the middle class in urban metropolis. The problem might get compounded with increasing consumer preferences for larger personal vehicles, fitted with highly energy-intensive power steering and air conditioning, leading to higher energy consumption and associated emissions.

Table 9.2

Energy Intensity and CO_2 Emission for an On-road Passenger Vehicle across all Modes of Road Transport in India (As of 2004-05)

Modes	*Energy Intensity (in MJ/passenger km)*	*CO_2 Emissions (in kg)*
Cars	0.864	0.058-0.064
Two-wheelers	0.476	0.032-0.036
Three-wheelers	0.580	0.039-0.043
Buses	0.137	0.009-0.0102

Note: MJ-Megajoule; CO_2 emissions have been computed for the uncertainty range of CEF factors provided in IPCC Guidelines, 2006.

Source: Calculated by the author using data on passenger traffic for 2004-05.

Increase in Freight Traffic

In the aftermath of economic reforms and industrialisation in the developing world coupled with globalisation, inter- and intra-city freight traffic are increasing with growing demand for increased speeds and reliability. Freight movement in developing countries is largely by road, although some countries have well-developed railway

6. Vehicle kilometre is the unit of vehicle traffic and indicates the total distance travelled by a vehicle. One vehicle km means one kilometre traversed by the vehicle. Usually, vehicle km is measured and considered on an annual basis. Passenger km is the unit of passenger traffic and is usually measured by multiplying the vehicle km by the occupancy ratio (number of occupants in the vehicle). One passenger km is also usually measured or considered annually.

networks. For instance, in China, while inland transport and railways contribute significantly to freight movement, the share of road transport is on the increase. Similarly in India, road is the dominant mode of transport and the share of railways is shrinking (this issue is discussed in greater detail further on). The share of inland water transport and coastal shipping in India is also insignificant. Furthermore, heavy-duty trucks used in India and most developing countries are largely two-axle vehicles which are not fuel efficient.[7] Additionally, most of these trucks are overloaded, and frequent detention at various checkpoints leaves the vehicles idling, adversely affecting both fuel efficiency and operational efficiency. This causes further increase in consumption of fuel and concomitant rise in CO_2 emissions.

Distorted Urban Transport Planning

Urban transport planning and markets in India and most of other developing countries are usually distorted with a strong inherent bias towards increased usage of personalised modes. For example, motorists are rarely charged the full costs of congestion, road space, parking and air pollution. Public policies usually tend to favour personalised modes and the bulk of public expenditure in most cities has been on expanding infrastructure (like highways, roads, flyovers, parking facilities and so on) to cater to the needs of these personalised modes (Sundar and Dhingra, 2008).

Structural Challenges in Modal Shifts (S)

Marginalisation of Public Transport

Between 1951 and 2006 the vehicle population grew at a compound annual growth rate (CAGR) of nearly 11 per cent. However, the share of buses in total registered vehicles has declined from 11.1 per cent in 1951 to 1.1 per cent in 2006.

---

7. Trucks on a single frame with two axles and dual rear wheels. Multi-axle trucks may consist of both single and more units. In case of multi-units, one unit is a tractor or straight truck power units.

This marginalisation of public bus transport reflects major sociological and economic changes related to increase in disposable income of urban households and changes in lifestyles, and so on. The demand for speed, service quality, convenience, flexibility and availability favoured adoption of private mode as the main mode of transport. In addition to this, government regulation and control have exacerbated the poor operational and financial performance of publicly owned transport undertakings, which are the main providers of bus transport services in the urban metropolis, resulting in increasing reliance on personalised private modes of passenger transport and marginalisation of public transport. Some major reasons for the poor performance of the public sector transport undertakings are the high staff cost and loss on account of low user charges which are not compensated for by state or central governments. Furthermore, operation of the public transport on economically unviable routes coupled with high rates of taxation exacerbates the problem of financial non-viability of public transport system in India. Figure 9.5 indicates the contribution of different taxes to the total operating cost of a bus.

Although buses are carrying 40-60 per cent of total trips in some large cities of India, their fleet is in want of modernisation and strengthening in order to reduce emissions. A good system of public transport is highly desirable since it provides more capacity at less marginal cost; produces less emission per passenger km travelled; and reduces congestion on roads by weaning away personal vehicle users.

Relative Decline in Rail Transport Share in Both Intra-city and Inter-city Passenger and Freight Traffic

Table 9.3 provides a summarised overview of the total road-based and rail-based passenger and freight traffic from 1971 to 2006. Although total population registered a growth of around 98 per cent during this period, absolute road-based passenger traffic increased from 210 billion passenger km to 4,252 billion passenger km in India, which represents an overwhelming growth of around 1,924 per cent at a CAGR of nearly 9.0 per cent per year. The absolute road-based

Figure 9.5

Contribution of Different Taxes to the Total Operating Cost of a Bus

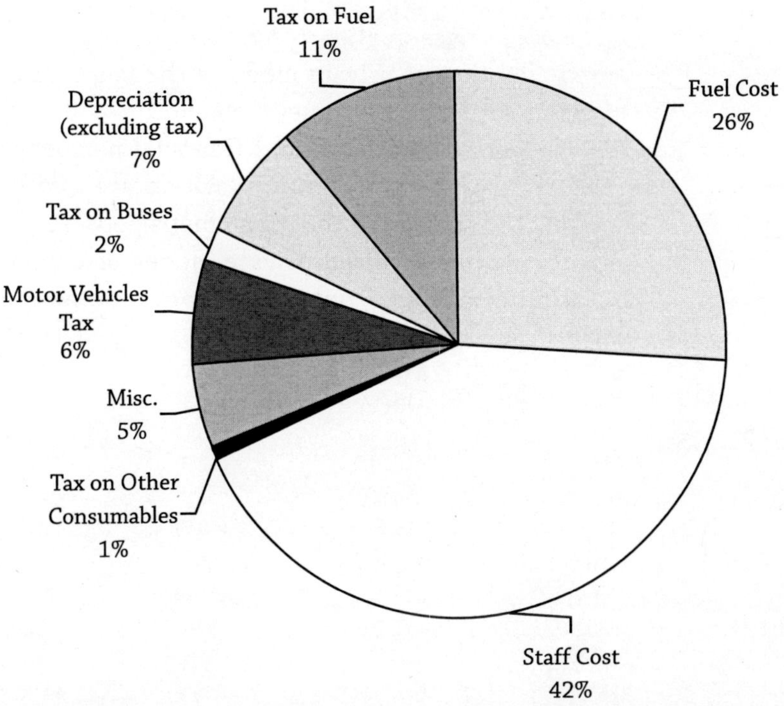

Source: Kharola and Tiwari, 2008.

freight traffic grew from 48 billion tonne km to 659 billion tonne km indicating a phenomenal growth of nearly 1,281 per cent at a CAGR of around 8 per cent per year. However, the rail-based passenger and freight traffic lost their shares to road-based passenger and freight traffic.

Railways are a relatively benign mode of transport as compared to road transport when considered in terms of energy intensity and emission. In this context, an empirical study carried out by Asian Institute of Transport Development (AITD, 2002) deserves special mention. The study made a comparative assessment of inter-city rail and road transport in India from perspectives of social and

Table 9.3

Road-based and Rail-based Passenger and Freight Traffic

Year	*Road-based Passenger Traffic (billion passenger km)*	*Rail-based Passenger Traffic*	*Road-based Freight Traffic (billion freight km)*	*Rail-based Freight Traffic*
1970-71	210.00 (64.0)	118.10 (36.0)	47.7 (30.1)	110.7 (69.9)
1980-81	541.80 (72.2)	208.60 (27.8)	90.9 (38.1)	147.7 (61.9)
1990-91	767.70 (72.2)	295.60 (27.8)	145.1 (38.1)	235.8 (61.9)
1999-2000	1831.60 (81.0)	430.70 (19.0)	467 (60.5)	305.2 (39.5)
2000-01	2075.50 (82.0)	457.70 (18.0)	494 (61.3)	312.4 (38.7)
2001-02	2413.10 (83.1)	1490.90 (16.9)	515 (60.7)	333.2 (39.3)
2002-03	2814.70 (84.5)	515.00 (15.5)	545 (60.7)	353.2 (39.3)
2003-04	3070.20 (85.0)	541.20 (15.0)	595 (61.0)	381.2 (39.0)
2004-05	3469.30 (85.8)	575.70 (14.2)	646 (61.3)	411.3 (38.7)
2005-06	4251.70 (87.4)	615.60 (12.6)	658.9 (60.0)	441.80 (40.0)

Note: *Figures in parenthesis indicate percentage share.

Source: Government of India, 2009.

environmental sustainability. The study observed that the energy consumption on different inter-city rail sections in the case of freight traffic varied between 10.28 and 25.01 per cent of the energy consumed by road transport in parallel stretches of state and national highway. In the case of passenger transport, the energy consumption on rail varied between 78.77 and 94.91 per cent of the energy consumed by road transport (Figures 9.6 and 9.7). Furthermore, land requirement for road corridor has been observed to be two and a half times that of rail corridor.

Figure 9.6

Energy Consumption: Inter-city Passenger Road and Rail

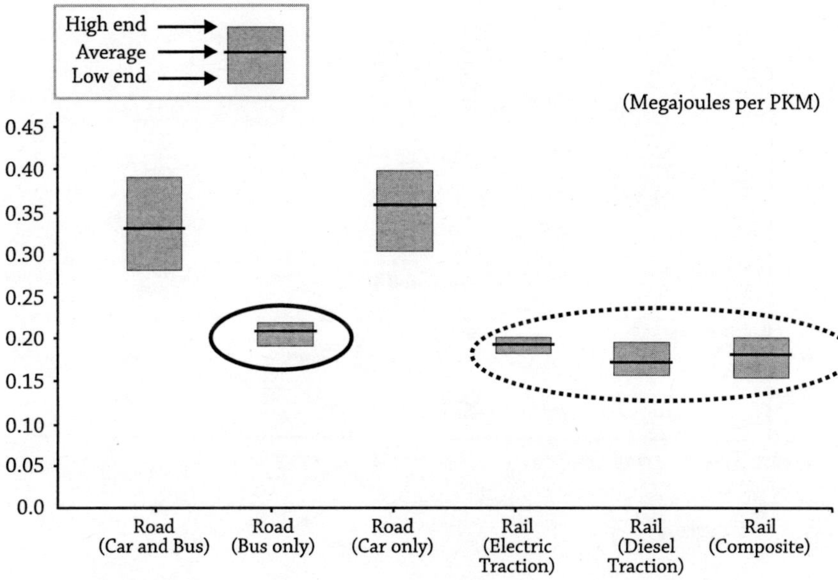

Source: AITD, 2002.

Challenges in Reducing Energy Intensity (I)

Poor Standards of Fuel Efficiency and Emission

Appropriate fuel-efficiency and vehicle emissions standards designed for new and in-use vehicles and well-designed and functional inspection and maintenance (I/M) programmes are important elements of an overall strategy to reduce vehicle emissions and air pollution.

Developed countries such as the US, Europe, Japan, Australia and South Korea have regulations for the automobile industry where the regulated metric involves either fuel economy of vehicles, fuel consumption of vehicles, CO_2 emission from vehicles or a combination of fuel economy and CO_2 emissions over a targeted period of time (Table 9.4). Among the developing countries, only China introduced regulations to improve fuel efficiency in 2005.

Figure 9.7

Energy Consumption: Inter-city Freight Road and Rail

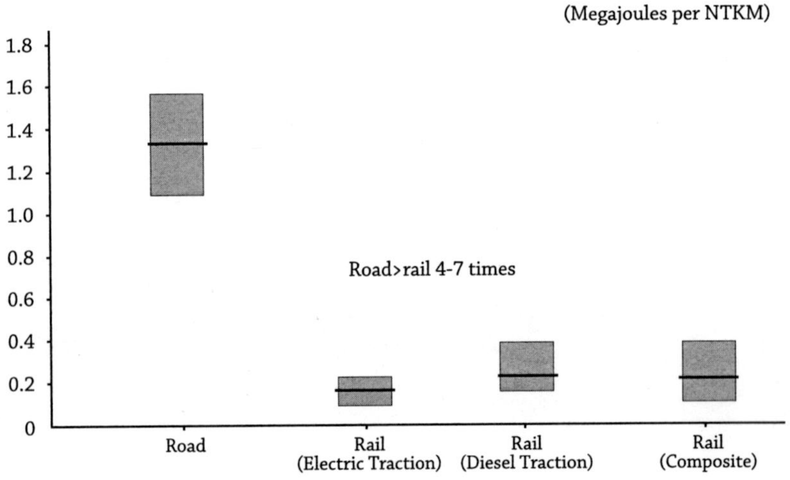

Source: AITD, 2002.

Table 9.4

Worldwide Automobile Efficiency or GHG Standards

Country/Region	*Regulated Metric*	*Expected Reduction in CO_2 per-distance Emissions**
European Union	CO_2 emissions (CO_2/km)	40% reduction, MY 2008-20
United States	Fuel economy (miles/gallon)	20% reduction, MY 2011-16
	GHG emissions (CO_2e/mile)	
Japan	Fuel economy (km/L)	19% reduction, MY 2010-15
China	Fuel consumption (L/100 km)	12% reduction, MY2008-15
California	GHG emissions (CO_2 e/mile)	25% reduction, MY 2008-16
Australia	Fuel consumption (L/100 km)	10% reduction, MY 2004-10
South Korea	Fuel economy (km/L)	13% reduction, MY 2012-15
	CO_2 emissions (CO_2/km)	

Note: * Expected reduction in CO_2 reduction pertains to different test driving cycles for different countries; MY stands for measurable year.

Source: Bandivadekar, 2009.

India is still in the process of designing fuel efficiency standards for motorised vehicles.

With regard to emissions standards, while India's two-wheeler standards are stricter than those in Europe, it lags behind Europe in respect of four-wheelers. Furthermore, the national roadmap for fuel quality and vehicle emission standards is selective and focuses only on the larger cities and neglects the rapidly motorising medium and small towns. Emission standards pan-India were introduced with Bharat Stage (BS) I (equivalent to Euro 1) in 2000. BS II (equivalent to Euro II) standards came into force in the country in 2005. BS III (equivalent to Euro III) standards were introduced in 2005 across 11 cities to be extended nationwide by 2010. BS IV (equivalent to Euro IV) standards are scheduled for introduction in 13 major and more polluted cities by 2010 but no date has yet been set for introducing Euro IV equivalent standards in the rest of India. With regard to inspection and maintenance system, the large population of personalised passenger vehicles in Indian metropolises is not yet covered by any mandatory requirement of periodic fitness certification. What exists in practice is a simple pollution under control (PUC) check which was introduced in 1991 for all on-road vehicles.

Price Distortions in Automobile Fuel

The phase of rapid expansion in the pace of growth of the Indian economy, particularly in the new millennium, coupled with the policy of keeping the retail selling prices of petrol and diesel shielded from fluctuation in international oil prices through regulation has generated perverse incentives and invariably led to an unabated increase in consumption of both fuels. High auto-fuel prices act as a signal to consumers that they need to take action to reduce consumption. Thus, removing that signal also removes the incentive to invest, for example, in more fuel-efficient vehicles, and makes consumers more vulnerable to future price increases. Furthermore, the continuance of universal insulation of auto-fuel prices from international oil price fluctuation usually tends to benefit the relatively well-off sections of passengers primarily in the densely populated cities as the propensity for personalised modes like cars tends to be considerably higher among the latter (see Bandyopadhyay, 2010a; 2010b).

Declining Share of Non-motorised Transport (NMT)

Non-motorised modes of transport such as walking and cycling have zero emissions. These have been in use in many developing countries including China, Colombia, Chile, the African continent and India. However, with easy availability of motorised transport and safety concerns regarding walking and cycling, there has been a marked shift away from non-motorised transport. Many cities rely on para-transit vehicles like auto-rickshaws and mini-buses to satisfy unmet travel demand. Generally, these vehicles are fuel inefficient and lead to higher emissions.

Challenges in Reducing Carbon Content of the Fuel (F)

Heavy Dependence on Petroleum

Among the sectors that use oil in India, transport has the largest share (Table 9.5). Moreover, nearly 96 per cent of the total commercial energy used in the transport sector comes from oil (Table 9.6). Given the fact that imported crude provides for more than 75 per cent of the refinery throughput for meeting domestic oil consumption in India, transport sector, in general, and road transport sector, in particular, are most exposed to volatility in international crude prices. Increasing volatility creates uncertainties, making it non-conducive for fresh investments to pour in, and often leads to delay in major investments in new oil production and refining capacity besides acting as a deterrent to investment in fuel-efficient car technology (see Bandyopadhyay, 2008; 2009b).

Table 9.5

Sectoral Distribution of Oil Use in India
(As Percentage Share of Total Oil Use across Sectors)

Year	*Industry*	*Transport*	*Agriculture*	*Commercial and Public Services*	*Residential Households*
1971	24.5	37.4	4.3	0.8	21.6
1990	22.9	45.1	0.4	3.1	23.8
2005	17.9	33.3	5.6	0.4	19.7

Note: The shortfall of the row sum from 100 is to be imputed to non-energy use of energy resources or use by other sectors.

Source: Adopted from Sengupta, 2007; originally computed using different volumes of *Energy Balances of Non-OECD Countries* published by IEA.

Table 9.6

Sector-wise Oil Application in India
(As Percentage of Total Final Commercial Energy Use in a Sector)

Year	*Industry*	*Transport*	*Agriculture*	*Commercial and Public Services*	*Residential Households*
1971	19.3	45.8	63.6	27.8	64.8
1990	17.0	88.9	4.7	47.2	79.6
2005	26.0	95.8	41.5	-	63.0

Source: Adopted from Sengupta, 2007; originally computed using different volumes of *Energy Balances of Non-OECD Countries* published by IEA.

Absence of Adequate Low-Carbon Substitutes

The substitutes for oil in urban road transport are currently inadequate and not always commercially viable. Although in 1998, the Supreme Court mandated conversion of all public buses in Delhi to compressed natural gas (CNG) and for subsequent conversion of all Government of India (GoI) vehicles to CNG, no roadmap has been constructed towards that end primarily due to a dearth of adequate natural gas supply. Until recently, the primary source of natural gas in India has been the offshore Western coast of Arabian Sea (South Bassein), which has also started deteriorating in terms of production. The pumping of natural gas by Reliance Industries Limited (RIL) and Oil and Natural Gas Corporation (ONGC) from the D-6 field in Krishna Godavari (KG) basin of Bay of Bengal has just begun (see Bandyopadhyay, 2009a) and it is only after adequate distribution network and infrastructure are put in place in all the cities for distribution of CNG can one expect the dependence on petroleum to come down considerably.

The government has also been encouraging the use of biofuels and has set a targeted blending of 20 per cent ethanol with gasoline by 2017 under the National Biofuel Policy. However, concerns related to the trade-offs that may arise with respect to availability of land, food-crop production, land-use changes and bio-diversity and, above all, availability of feedstock remain in order to raise the blending to the targeted level. In addition, the ability of biofuel to reduce GHGs is still contested by scientists around the world. Electricity is the cleanest and cheapest fuel for transport (running cost is much lower compared to conventional gasoline- or diesel-powered vehicles) but it is yet to draw adequate appeal in terms of commercial viability due to high upfront cost involved in purchase and replacement of the batteries, lack of adequate mileage and dearth of adequate charging facilities. Furthermore, electricity produced from thermal power plants running largely on inferior quality coal does not save in terms of CO_2 emissions and thus the electricity generated cannot be considered as a low-carbon source.

Institutions and Governance-related Challenges

Transport planning and management in urban metropolis necessitates a holistic and coordinated approach. However, in most developing countries including India, there is a plethora of impediments to a coordinated approach, mainly due to dearth of appropriate institutional arrangements and linkages (Sundar and Dhingra, 2008). The authorities and associated responsibilities pertaining to urban transport planning and management are often fragmented and divided between and within the state and city governments. Furthermore, these authorities also lack the necessary power, resources and capacity to address problems of congestion, air pollution and GHG emissions. A particular challenge in institutional development for sustainable urban transport in developing countries is posed by the large share of para-transit modes in public transport.[8] These modes operate in the (semi) informal sector and are not easy to integrate in governmental programmes for fleet renewal to reform the transport sector in order to make it less carbon intensive.[9]

Addressing the Challenges

Urban transport is considered to be a major plank for pro-poor economic growth especially in developing countries like India. Therefore, putting a cap on urban transport growth is neither feasible nor desirable. As India continues to grow on a higher trajectory, the demand for urban transport will also increase concomitantly. Thus, the key challenge that the policy makers in India are encountering is to decouple economic and social development from the inevitable increase in energy consumption and CO_2 emissions that arises due to rapid growth of urban transport.

A standalone policy of reducing GHG emissions (CO_2 in particular) from urban transport sector may not appeal significantly to policy makers and other stakeholders because the cost involved is considerably high. Initiatives to restrain CO_2 emissions from urban transport consequently need to be aligned closely with overall strategies to reform the sector and should essentially be recognised as co-benefits rather than as a primary goal. In view of this, a meeting was held in Bellagio in May 2009[10] leading to the formulation of a common policy framework on sustainable low-carbon urban transport for developing countries aimed primarily at the urban road transport. The framework recognised an integrated multi-pronged approach based on co-benefits and underscored sector-wide re-orientation of transport sector combining policies and

8. In South Asia, this includes the motorised three-wheeled rickshaws, locally assembled jeepneys and buses built around imported second-hand truck engines in Philippines and the Bemo in Indonesia.

9. Because they operate in the informal sector, they often do not keep formal books, have formal franchises or pay taxes on a regular basis which can be a guarantee to benefit from financial assistance programmes.

10. *http://www.sutp.org/slocat/about/bellagio-process/targets-and-progress/*

measures aimed at: (a) avoiding or reducing travel or need to travel; (b) shifting to more environment friendly or energy-efficient modes; and (c) improving efficiency of motorised modes. This approach is more popularly known as avoid-shift-improve framework. The next few paragraphs are devoted to a discussion of the instruments and measures pertaining to this framework.

Reduce Travel or Need to Travel

Integration of Land Use and Urban Transport Planning

Integrating land use planning with transport planning is a key to reducing GHG emissions in urban metropolis. Travel can be reduced when various forms of land use such as residential houses, shops and public services are mixed and located in close proximity of one another. Density of an area is crucial for emission reduction. Where low density leads to heavy dependence on private vehicles and higher energy demand, areas with higher density reduce travel needs and emissions. Demand for transport in high-density centres in urban metropolis is more easily served by public transport as it is cost-effective due to reasonable load factor or occupancy ratio. Instances of such integration of land use and transport planning can be drawn from the city of Toronto in Canada.[11] Proper land use planning can also provide for pedestrian footways and cycle paths and encourage the use of NMT modes.

Promoting Use of Alternatives to Travel

Use of communication and information technologies can help avoid or reduce the need to travel. For instance, introduction of 'Easy Bill' facility in Delhi and some other cities has helped citizens pay most of their utility bills at nearby centres at convenient hours. Similarly, in Bangalore, the Government of Karnataka has set up one-stop facility for citizens to access information and pay all government

11. Driven by increasing concerns regarding climate change, the City of Toronto recognised the importance of transit in its Official Plan called the Toronto Transit City, which said, "No new roads will be built in Toronto. Instead, all growth in travel demand is to be carried on transit" (More details available at: *http://www.transitcity.ca/media/TransitCity_fullreport.pdf*).

and municipal bills. Some corporate organisations, particularly in developed countries, have 'work from home' programmes which reduce travel demand. However, in order to implement these initiatives universally and successfully, well-knit information and communication networks should be put in place on a priority basis.

Regulatory Instruments

Regulatory instruments can be used to discourage travel or deny access to certain traffic or vehicles. Some regulatory measures that already exist especially in developed countries include:

Physical restraint measures: City authorities can implement physical restraints like restricting access for certain private vehicles. One such measure is the restriction on plying of vehicles on certain days depending on their registration plate number. This has been widely implemented in Athens, Manila, Mexico City and Seoul, among others. The benefits of this measure include reduction in congestion, increase in speed and saving in fuel consumption. However, the measures may not be without leakages, as evinced by the example of Hoy no Circulan (a day without a car) in Mexico City.[12]

Traffic management measures: Traffic management measures are used to smoothen traffic flows, improve fuel efficiency and reduce emissions. Among traffic signal systems, the most efficient is the area traffic control system where signals are coordinated across a whole network. In developed countries, traffic management has achieved emission reduction by around 2-5 per cent. In developing countries, this measure can help achieve higher reduction in fuel consumption and emissions. It has also been estimated that effective land use planning together with better traffic management schemes [like Intelligent Transportation System (ITS)] can bring about energy savings of 20-30 per cent for public transport (Dalkmann

12. Towards early 1990s, Mexico City started a programme called 'Hoy no Circulan' under which cars were not be allowed to be driven for a day in a week depending on the last number of the license plate. However, World Bank research (Eskeland and Feyzioglu, 1995) indicates that this measure was not successful in saving fuel consumption. The outcome was just the opposite, as the measure led to an increase in purchase of second-hand cars with a different last number on the license plate. This example shows how 'leakages' may occur if measures are implemented without careful planning to anticipate possible outcomes.

and Brannigan, 2007) due to better planned trips and smooth vehicle movement. For example, Hong Kong's ITS project after its completion in 2010 is expected to modernise the traffic operations on major highways, road tunnels and urban roads.[13]

Regulation of parking: Restriction of parking space supply can make car use unattractive and encourage modal shift. Planning authorities can also involve employers and commercial establishments in reducing private parking space reserved for their employees or customers. Citywide initiatives involving private entities are likely to be more successful compared to restrictions imposed only on publicly provided parking.

Speed restrictions: To reduce GHG emissions, governments may prescribe minimum and maximum speed limits for vehicles.

Inspection, maintenance and certification: An effective inspection and certification programme coupled with driver training and adequate maintenance can bring about 2-17 per cent reduction in fuel consumption and GHG emissions (ADB, 2006).

Economic Instruments

The primary objective of economic instruments is to discourage the use of private vehicles or encourage more efficient use of transport through levy of charges or taxes. Various economic instruments are discussed below:

Road pricing and congestion charging: In general, road pricing increases the cost of running a vehicle and thereby encourages the use of alternate modes. Implementing agencies usually have two options: (a) introducing national road pricing where charges are applied on long-distance highway use, and (b) introducing local road pricing schemes that cover only city-centre areas. To reduce peak period vehicle traffic, road pricing rates can be fixed at a higher rate for certain periods. The scheme could be highly effective in reducing GHG emissions. Interestingly, Delhi High Court also came out with a ruling in February 2010 in support of congestion charges for car owners passing through congested areas of the city (Garg, 2010).

---

13. For more, go to: *http://www.roadtraffic-technology.com/projects/hong-kong.*

Fuel taxation: Fuel taxes can increase the price of travel and consequently affect individual travel behaviour. This can produce desired results as owners make efforts to reduce the number of vehicle kilometres travelled. Since fuel taxation is proportional to fuel consumption, this could provide an incentive to purchase fuel-efficient vehicles. Either way, it will help in reducing GHG emissions. However, due care should be taken to remove any unjustifiable distortions that may exist in the fuel taxation system that discriminates against any particular fuel, leading to pricing anomalies or generation of perverse incentives.

Vehicle taxation: Vehicle taxes are regarded as an 'access fee' to use the road network. Charges vary with vehicle type, vehicle size or emissions and noise levels. If tax rates are differentiated according to fuel consumption, this will encourage sale of fuel-efficient vehicles. However, this tax does not necessarily ensure efficient operation of the vehicles. Additional measures would therefore be required to promote energy-efficient vehicles through levy of fuel taxation. Due care needs to be taken to ensure that the axe of vehicle tax does not fall on public transport system as that would frustrate the very objective of moving towards a low-carbon transport.

Parking pricing: This instrument increases the cost of using a vehicle by raising the cost of parking. This can be expected to substantially reduce parking demand compared to free parking regime.

Information Instruments

Information instruments include awareness campaigns, mobility management and driver education and training. Marketing of sustainable transport system requires public awareness and acceptance of the negative impact of certain transport systems and practices. Therefore, there is a need for information instruments to spread these messages. For instance, Colombia and Mexico have implemented 'car-free days,' banning cars from entering the city on certain days. In India, the city of Ahmedabad has also initiated car-free days. This can be coupled with promotion of alternate mode choices such as public transport, cycling or walking. Education through schools or dissemination of information through places of employment can also be useful in raising awareness. Improving fuel efficiency is also possible through education and training of drivers, which facilitates behavioural change with regard to speed, braking and acceleration, engine idling, carrying capacity and vehicle condition (vehicle age, oil and air filter, maintenance of engine, tyres). Estimates show that fuel savings through this measure are in the range of 10-15 per cent (Dalkmann and Brannigan, 2007).

Shift to Environment Friendly Modes

Improve the Share of Public Transport

The expansion of public transport in the form of large-capacity buses, light rail transit and suburban rail or metro is a feasible option for transport sector (Kahn *et al.*, 2007). The IPCC recognises the preservation and augmentation of the market shares of low-emitting collective transport modes as a worldwide mitigation option. However, public transport should be accessible, attractive, affordable and reliable if it is to replace private vehicles.

Improvement of public transport is possible through expansion of systems or services and/or improvement in operation of systems and services pertaining to public transport. The expansion of services can include dedicated lanes, express bus services and local bus services. Operational improvements may include splitting of routes, increased vehicle frequency, coordination of routes through integrated ticketing. Services may also be improved through provision of passenger amenities.

The bus rapid transit (BRT) system, Transmilenio, in Bogotá, Colombia, is one of the most successful models of BRT passenger transport system.[14] There is no specific definition of an ideal BRT

14. Transmilenio in Bogotá consists of a BRT system which is being implemented gradually since the end of 2001. It currently transports more than 2 million passengers daily. Transmilenio reduces emissions per passenger trip compared to the traditional transport system due to the use of new and larger buses, mode switching due to increased attractiveness of public transport (around 10% of Transmilenio would have used taxis or passenger cars in absence of the system) and improved bus occupancy rates as a result of a centrally managed vehicle dispatch (Grutter, 2007; 2008).

system. Some features of BRT systems include exclusive right of way lanes, rapid boarding and alighting, free transfers between lines, pre-board fare collection and fare verification, enclosed stations, clear route maps, real-time information displays, automatic vehicle location technology to manage vehicle movements, modal integration at stations, effective reform of the existing institutional structures for public transit, clean vehicle technologies and excellence in marketing and customer services (Grutter, 2007). Table 9.7 delineates the broad characteristics and CO_2 impact estimates for selected international BRT systems.

In India, the first BRT corridor was opened in Delhi. Surveys among the users of the BRT indicated general satisfaction with the service provided despite the shortcomings in the original design and its implementation. In Ahmedabad, the city residents have embraced their new Janmarg BRT system; around 18,000 daily passengers use Janmarg to commute to work, to school and elsewhere. Janmarg uses innovative central median stations pulled away from the junctions. Bus stations feature passive solar design, an inexpensive way to keep stations naturally cool. The city is making continued efforts to be a leader in sustainable transport, incorporating high-quality pedestrian facilities in some corridors, as well as bicycle lanes.

Promote Non-motorised Transport (NMT)

Shorter trips are best performed by NMT. These modes can be promoted through provision of cycling and walking tracks and through road safety measures; appropriate pricing of individual vehicle use and fuels; regulation of polluting motorised modes; and use of information and awareness campaigns. In this light, in a judgment dated 10 February 2010 (in response to petitions filed against the cap of 99,000 three-wheeler cycle rickshaw licences imposed by the Municipal Corporation of Delhi in 1997), the Chief Justice bench of the Delhi High Court proactively saved an important non-motorised mode from near extinction by removing the restriction on the number of licences that can be issued to the rickshaw pullers. The bench also stated that confiscation and scrapping of cycle rickshaws are against the law.[15]

The High Court bench also mandated the formation of a special task force to explore all questions pertaining to road traffic in the city with the aim of minimising congestion, reducing pollution levels from vehicles and ensuring equitable access to all classes of vehicles that ply on roads (including NMT such as bicycles and cycle rickshaws) (Staff Reporter, 2010).

Shifting Freight Traffic from Road to Energy-efficient Modes

One of the most pressing needs in the urban freight transport sector in developing nations including India is to increase the share of railways and inland transport in freight traffic. Although large investments are being made in developing alternate modes in many developing countries in order to augment the carrying capacity, these investments are not always coupled with endeavours to make these modes cost and energy efficient, attractive and capable of meeting consumer requirements. In this context, adequate insights can be gained from the Marco Polo model of freight shift in modal transportation in Europe (Box 9.1), which shows how targeted policy interventions including fiscal incentives can make the desired low-carbon-oriented inter-modal freight shifts possible.

Box 9.1

Marco Polo Model

The Marco Polo programme (Marco Polo I) was launched in 2003 to improve the sustainability and efficiency of the transport sector. The programme provides subsidy to transport service operators to facilitate a shift from the road to more environment-friendly modes of transportation, such as short sea shipping, rail and inland waterways or to a combination of modes of transport in which road journeys are as short as possible. The idea is to assist supporting intermodal freight transport initiatives and alternatives to road-

contd...

15. Delhi High Court ruling in the two cases: Manushi Sangathan, Delhi *versus* Government of India and others, WP (C) No. 4572/2007; Initiative for Transportation and Development Programmes *versus* Municipal Corporation of Delhi and others, WP (C) No. 8580/2009.

...contd...

only transport in the early stages until they become commercially viable. The subsidy provided was at the rate of 1euro per 500 tonne km. shifted off the road. The programme had expected to shift the expected aggregate increase in international road freight traffic of

12 billion tonne kms. (btkm.) per year to cleaner modes during the programme period 2003-2010. It was also estimated that every 1 euro of subsidy to Marco Polo would generate at least 6 euros in social and environmental benefits.

Marco Polo II, which pertains to the period 2007 to 2013, is more ambitious than its predecessor. It has a larger budget and supports two new types of actions (the motorways of the seas and traffic avoidance measures) over an extended area that includes neighbouring non-EU countries. In all, Marco Polo provides support for 5 distinct types of action which are as follows:

Modal shift actions: The aim is to shift as much freight as economically meaningful under current market conditions from road to short sea shipping, rail and inland waterways.

Catalyst actions: The goal here is to change the way non-road freight transport is conducted in the EU. Support will be provided to innovative proposals aimed at overcoming structural market barriers in European freight transport.

Common learning actions: The objective here is to enhance knowledge in the freight logistics sector and foster advanced methods and procedures of cooperation in the freight market.

Motorways of the sea actions: This measure is intended to shift freight from long road distances to a combination of short sea shipping and other modes of transport.

Traffic avoidance actions: The objective here is to integrate transport into production logistics. This should lead to a reduced freight transport demand by road with a direct impact on emissions. It is emphasised that actions of this type shall not adversely affect either output or the labour workforce.

More details available at: *http://ec.europa.eu/transport/marcopolo/home/home_en.htm*

Table 9.7

Characteristics and CO_2 Impact Estimates for Select BRT Systems

City	*Reported Data and Estimates from Studies*						*IEA Estimates based on Car-Taxi Vehicle km Reduction in Studies*	
	BRT Line Distance (km)	*Percentage Shift from Car/Taxi to BRT*	*Vehicle Travel Reduction (million km)*	*Million Vehicle km Saved per km BRT*	*CO_2 Reduction per km per year (in tonnes)*	*Total CO_2 Reduction per Year (in tonnes)*	*Calculated CO_2 Savings (tonnes/ year)*	*As a Percentage of Reported CO_2 Savings*
Bogotá	84	9	435.0	5.2	2940	247000	83520	34
Mexico City	20	6	23.0	1.2	900	18000	4416	25
Pereira	30	16	54.5	1.8	900	27000	10464	39
Chongqing	82	21	495.3	6.0	3171	260000	95098	38

Source: IEA, 2009a, table 5.16.

Improving Vehicle Technology and Energy Efficiency

Variation in GHG emissions is contingent upon the nature of fuels and technologies used. Thus, technology solutions for vehicles usually underscore two possible areas of improvement with respect to GHG emissions: (a) reducing the carbon content of fuel (say by altering the mix of fuels actually used) and/or (b) influencing the intensity with which fuels are used.

This could be achieved by promoting and providing incentives for use of road friendly and fuel-efficient vehicles by introducing appropriate fuel efficiency standards; making superior quality fuel adequately available for transport vehicles; and putting in place appropriate regulatory policies to check fuel adulteration. In order to tap the full potential of technological improvements especially in passenger transport, these measures should be supplemented with policy instruments that focus on promoting modal shifts and reducing overall travel time.[16]

Furthermore, electric vehicles (EVs) and hybrid electric vehicles (HEV) should be promoted in India on a priority basis given that they are more cost-effective and cleaner than diesel- and gasoline-powered vehicles. This is despite the fact that the electricity generation process in India will take a lot of time to become less GHG intensive. In fact EVs are already being produced on a mass scale in India in the form of two-wheeled bikes and scooters and the four-wheeled light duty vehicles are expected to catch up soon. Globally, however, HEVs (using both petrol and electric propulsion system) are expected to capture the market sooner as compared to EVs since these vehicles do not require refuelling or charging infrastructure. Although both EVs and HEVs have a great potential in India, policy support is crucial for making them cost-competitive. Expanded use of EVs and

16. However, it should be recognised that the overall growth in travel and freight activity, which increases at a rapid pace in developing countries, may offset the gains from new technology or technological upgradation. This rebound effect occurs in particular if automobile fuel prices are regulated, leading to a pure income effect of lowered fuel cost that might offset any savings in consumption or reduction in emissions. This is true for India also, where the high-carbon automobile fuel prices remain within the regulated domain under administered prices.

HEVs will require a better understanding of consumer needs and desires. Measures to influence greater penetration could include fiscal and purchase incentives apart from influencing the driving range that is at present a serious constraint especially with electric two-wheelers and four-wheelers. Moreover, continuous support needs to be provided for research, development and demonstration so as to reduce battery cost and ensure adequate supply of materials for battery manufacture. Industry and governments must also work in tandem towards prioritising international collaboration that can facilitate research programmes aimed at accelerated deployment of smart grids and vehicle-grid interface for fuelling electric vehicles.[17]

Recent Initiatives by Indian Government towards Urban Low-Carbon Transport

The Indian government has taken a number of national policy initiatives that recognise some components of the avoid-shift-improve framework in order to address some of the challenges described in the preceding section. Box 9.2 provides a snapshot of these initiatives.

In terms of financing initiatives to bring about changes at the local level with support of strategic plans and programmes at the national level, the Jawaharlal Nehru National Urban Renewal Mission (JNNURM) in India provides a great example. JNNURM provides financial assistance as soft loans, grant-cum-loans or grants to urban local bodies and parastatal bodies *via* state-level nodal agencies in return for formulating city development plans (CDPs) and detailed project reports for urban infrastructure development. Furthermore, grants for urban buses have recently been made available, subject to the set-up of Dedicated Urban Transport Funds at state and city levels (Box 9.3).

17. The paragraph draws largely on IEA, 2009b and Chattopadhyay, 2010.

Box 9.2

Indian Government Initiatives that Address Some Components of Avoid-Shift-Improve Framework

National Urban Transport Policy (NUTP), 2006

- Aims to integrate land use and transport planning
- Facilitates investment in and promotion of public transport and encourages non-motorised modes
- Develops transport projects focussed on equitable allocation of road space
- Promotes clean vehicles
- Aims to raise resources through innovative financing mechanisms
- Focuses on building capacities

National Action Plan on Climate Change (NAPCC), 2008

- Suggests early introduction of fuel economy standards
- Promotes investments in high-capacity public transport systems
- Suggests introducing transport pricing measures to influence purchase of vehicles on the basis of their energy efficiency
- Envisages a ban on abandoning old vehicles, fixing responsibility on the last owner of the vehicle to handover the vehicle at the end of its life to specific collection centres to be nominated by the government
- Encourages setting up of demonstration centres to take up recycling of vehicles, especially two-wheelers
- Encourages energy R&D in Indian railways
- Promotes use of coastal shipping and inland waterways, encourages rail-based movement instead of long-distance road-based movement.

Source: *http://pmindia.nic.in/climate_change.htm; www.urbanindia.nic.in/policies/TransportPolicy.pdf*

Box 9.3

Transport Funds in India

Examples of local transport funds in action can be seen in India, where recently, two urban areas have adopted such an approach. In Surat, vehicle taxes, parking charges and advertisement fees are fed into a dedicated urban transport fund, which is used to support its urban mobility plan, including the expansion of bus services and modification of three-wheelers to power on CNG. In Pimpri-Chinchwad, a 130 km. BRT network is being developed through an urban transport fund, funded by fares, monthly passes, advertisement and land-related taxes (e.g., development rights around the BRT corridor and property tax). India has also initiated the JNNURM, which at national level provides assistance to megacities in their efforts to improve urban infrastructure. Sustainable transport is one focus of this ambitious scheme. The philosophy behind the JNNURM is one of cost sharing between national and local level, in design, construction and operation of infrastructure. Recently, as part of the Indian government's economic stimulus package, a one-time assistance grant of $58 billion has been provided to the states under the framework of the JNNURM for the purchase of urban buses. This provision is subject to various conditions, including the setting up of a dedicated Urban Transport Fund at both the state and the city level. Revenue sources suggested for the Fund at state level include sales tax on petrol, vehicle registration fees, renewal fees for driving licences, congestion taxes and green taxes. The Fund at the city level includes betterment levies on land, parking fees, property development taxes and advertisement revenue.

Source: Leather, 2009.

Conclusion

It is indeed encouraging to observe that many of the potential policies and measures under avoid-shift-improve framework are already well known and have been tested in specific countries and cities in the developing or developed world and can be relatively easily replicated or scaled up. Indian policy making, both at the national and sub-national level, has also internalised some components of this approach. However, the financial, technological and institutional resources are yet to be fully reoriented towards an integrated and holistic avoid-shift-improve framework.

An important issue that deserves attention is that climate change does not seem to be the key driver of transport policies and projects in developing countries. This is because the potential financial earnings from GHG reduction tend to be significantly lower than other earnings or cost savings associated with a good transport policy or project that addresses local benefits, such as reduced traffic congestion and air pollution. Thus, these local negative spillovers still play a much bigger role in development of transport polices and investments than climate change mitigation.

In this context, it should be recognised that transport policies and programmes can have: (a) benefits: the primary goal of policies and project (e.g., reduced traffic congestion); (b) primary co-benefits: other benefits that directly result from transport policies or projects (e.g., GHG and air pollution reduction); or (c) secondary co-benefits: benefits that indirectly result from transport policies or project (e.g., reduced health impact and costs from air pollution). A holistic implementation of the avoid-shift-improve approach will be able to foster a synergy of these benefits and variegated co-benefits. But the implications of benefits and co-benefits may be different for different nations depending on the initial condition or the state of affairs under which such approach is being implemented. Thus, there is no 'one-size fits all' kind of tailor-made solution that could be applied universally. It is instead essential to adopt a needs-based combination of policies. For instance, in developing cities that are dominated by a large number of old, highly polluting vehicles, policies focusing on improvement based on technological solutions tend to have relatively high co-benefits. Similarly, in densely populated cities in developing countries that are yet to develop a strong planning capacity, planning instruments such as efficient mix of land use-transport-environment can bring about higher co-benefits. Likewise, in developing countries where the lion's share of pollution and emission is attributed to freight transport, regulatory and planning instruments targeting the freight sector can bring relatively large and immediate co-benefits. These examples should not, however, be taken to imply that other instruments or policies pertaining to the avoid-shift-improve approach are of lesser importance.

The fundamental point is that a minimum essential level of all the components or policies pertaining to this approach need to be implemented at the first instance, but depending on the state of affairs or specific needs in some countries or cities, particular components need to be given more or less attention. The speed and level of implementation would be largely contingent upon concomitant efforts made in developing awareness levels among the masses; reforms and coordination in nature of policies and institutions; invoking a high degree of transparency and accountability; and finally, the efforts undertaken in augmenting capacity and resources.

Institutional development in support of low-carbon urban transport is in particular crucial and includes: (a) clarification of institutional mandates at all geographical levels (local, sub-national, national, regional and global); (b) strengthening of institutional capacities within all sectors (government, civil society, academia and private sector); and (c) improved coordination and cooperation between different sectors at, and between, different geographical levels. The requirement of improved coordination applies significantly to integration of land-use and transport planning, and should essentially be directed towards development of comprehensive transport systems, rather than individual, *ad hoc* projects.

Furthermore, private sector participation in the provision of low-carbon transport products and services needs to be encouraged as the private sector is better at mobilising investments required to support the implementation of low-carbon transport policies. Experiences from developed countries indicate the importance of a transparent and predictable regulatory framework to promote private sector involvement. Therefore, in order to facilitate increased private sector participation, appropriate regulatory frameworks need to be developed in the first place. The same applies to the civil society which can help mobilise support for policy development and implementation, follow-up of policy commitments made by governments, and flag problems before they become unmanageable. The absence of effective and transparent public consultation mechanisms will ultimately slow down decision making and its implementation and might reduce the rate at which behavioural changes are adopted.

Developing countries like India and China should be playing a key role in applying this co-benefits approach and making their transport system sustainable and low-carbon based through a combination of policy instruments, institutional capacity development, appropriate pricing mechanisms and mobilisation of financial resources. However, in order to implement co-benefits approach, it should also be integrated in a more structured and quantified manner in policy analysis and feasibility studies of programmes and projects. This is more likely to happen if co-benefits are fully recognised and internalised in post-2012 climate agreement.

References

Asian Development Bank (2006). *Energy Efficiency and Climate Change Considerations for On-road Transport in Asia*. Philippines.

———. (2008). *Clean Energy Financing Partnership Facility: Semi Annual Progress Report, January-June*. Philippines. Available at: *http://www.adb.org/Documents/reports/CEFPF/CEFPF-Semiannual-Progress-Report.pdf*

Asian Institute of Transport Development (AITD) (2002). *Environmental and Social Sustainability of Transport: Comparative Study of Rail and Road*. New Delhi.

Bandivadekar, A. (2009). "Review of Fuel Economy/Greenhouse Gas Standards Worldwide", Presentation at the *Global Fuel Economy Initiative Symposium*. New Delhi. November 25.

Bandyopadhyay, K.R. (2008). "OPEC"s Price-making Power", *Economic and Political Weekly* 43(46): 18-21.

———. (2009a). "Adding KGs to GDP", *the Financial Express*, 4 December.

———. (2009b). "What will oil do in 2010?", *the Financial Express*, December 30.

———. (2010a). "Fossil Fuel Subsidy Reform in India", *Policy Brief* 45. January. New Delhi: Research and Information System for Developing Countries. Available at: *www.ris.org.in/pb45.pdf*

———. (2010b). "Crude Logic Lies in Decontrol", *The Financial Express*, February 4.

Basu, Agnimirh (2009). "Unorganised Players give e-bike a Bad Name", *Down to Earth*, August 16-31.

Chattopadhyay, Vivek (2010). "e Driven", *Down to Earth*, February 1-15. Delhi: Centre for Science and Environment

Dalkmann, H. and C. Brannigan (2007). "Transport and Climate Change", Module 5e in *Sustainable Transport: A Sourcebook for Policymakers in Developing Cities.* Germany: GTZ. Available at: *http://www.sutp.org.*

Environment Pollution (Control and Prevention) Authority (2009). "Learning from Practice: Examples of Fiscal Reform in Cities to Deal with Pollution and Congestion", *Briefing paper* 2b. February. Government of Delhi.

Eskeland, G.S. and T. Feyzioglu (1995). *Rationing Can Backfire: The Day "Without a Car" in Mexico City.* December. Washington DC: World Bank

Frost and Sullivan (2010). *Voice of Indian Automotive Customers 2009: Evaluation of Power Train Technologies in Vehicles.* February. Mumbai.

Garg, Abhinav (2010). "Delhi High Court Moots Congestion Fee on Cars", *The Times of India,* February 11.

Government of India (2009). *Road Transport Yearbook 2006-07.* New Delhi: Ministry of Shipping, Road Transport and Highways.

Grutter, Jurg M. (2008). "CDM Transport Projects Up and Coming", *JIKO Info* 6 (3): 1-6.

———. (2007). "CDM in the Transport Sector", Module 5d in *Sustainable Transport: A Sourcebook for Policymakers in Developing Cities.* Germany: GTZ. Available at: *http://www.sutp.org*

Huizenga, C. and S. Bakker (2009). "Applicability of Post 2012 Climate Instruments to the Transport Sector", *Draft Interim Synthesis Consultants Report.* December. Philippines: Asian Development Bank.

International Energy Agency (IEA) (2007a). *CO_2 Emissions from Fuel Combustion: 1971-2005.* Paris: IEA.

———. (2007b). *World Energy Statistics and Balances.* Paris: IEA.

———. (2007c). *CO_2 Emissions from Fuel Combustion: 1971-2005.* Paris: IEA.

———. (2007d). *World Energy Outlook.* Paris: IEA.

———. (2008). *World Energy Outlook.* Paris: IEA.

———. (2009). *Transport Energy and CO_2: Moving Towards Sustainability.* Paris: IEA.

———. (2009a). *Technology Roadmap: Electric and Plug-in Hybrid Vehicles (EV/PHEV).* Paris: IEA.

Kahn, R., Shigeki Kobayashi, Michel Beuthe, Jorge Gasca, David Greene, David S. Lee, Yasunori Muromachi, Peter J. Newton, Steven Plotkin, Daniel Sperling, Ron Wit and Peter J. Zhou (2007). "Transport and its Infrastructure", in Metz, B., O.R. Davidson, P.R. Bosch, R. Dave and L.A. Meyer (eds.) *Climate Change 2007: Mitigation.* Contribution of Working Group III to the Fourth Assessment Report of the Intergovernmental Panel on Climate Change (IPCC). Switzerland: IPCC.

Kharola B.S. and G. Tiwari (2008). "Urban Public Transport Systems: Are the Taxation Policies Congenial for their Survival and Growth", *Economic and Political Weekly* 43 (41): 41-7, October.

Leather, James (2009). "Rethinking Transport and Climate Change", *Draft Sustainable Development Working Paper.* September. Philippines: Asian Development Bank.

Reporter, Staff (2010). "Task Force to Find Solution to Delhi's Traffic Woes", *The Hindu,* February 11.

Schipper, L., C M-Lilliu and Roger Gorham (2000). *Flexing the Link between Transport and Greenhouse Gas Emissions: A Path for the World Bank.* June. Paris: IEA.

Sengupta, R. (2007). "High Economic Growth, Equity and Sustainable Energy Development of India", *Discussion Paper Series* 213. December. Japan: Research Institute of Economics and Business Administration, Kobe University. Available from: *http://www.rieb.kobe-u.ac.jp/academic/ra/dp/English/dp213.pdf.*

Sundar, S. and C. Dhingra (2008). "Reducing Transport CO_2 Emissions in Emerging Economies", Paper presented at the *Second Annual Conference of the International Transport Forum*. Leipzig, Germany.

Timilsina, G. and A. Shrestha (2009). "Why have CO_2 Emissions Increased in the Transport Sector in Asia? Underlying Factors and Policy Options", *Policy Research Working Paper* 5098. Washington DC: World Bank.

United Nations Environment Programme (UNEP) (2009). *CDM Pipeline.* Risø. December 1. Denmark: UNEP. Available at: *www.cdmpipeline.org*

World Bank (2008). *Clean Technology Fund.* Washington DC. Available at: *http://siteresources.worldbank.org/INTCC/Resources/Clean_Technology_Fund_paper_June_9_final.pdf*

———. (2009). *Transport Lending Trends 1996–2007.* Washington DC. Available at: *http://go.worldbank.org/KM9OPODLQ0*

World Business Council on Sustainable Development (WBCSD) (2004). *Mobility 2030: Meeting the Challenges to Sustainability.* USA.

Bibliography of Transport Studies

Abeyratne, Ruwantissa (2012). *Strategic Issues in Air Transport: Legal, Economic and Technical Aspects.* New York: Springer.

Anbalagan, P. (2012). *Urban Development and Sustainable Transport*. New Delhi.

Asariotis, Regina and Hassiba Benamara (eds.) (2012). *Maritime Transport and the Climate Change Challenge*. New York: Routledge.

Asbjørnslett, Bjørn Egil, Inge Norstad and Øyvind Berle (2012). *Risk-Based Design of Maritime Transport Systems*. Springer.

Banister, David (ed.) (2012). *Transport Policy and the Environment*. New York: Routledge.

———. (2012). *Unsustainable Transport: City Transport in the New Century*. New York: Routledge.

———. (2011). *Transport and Urban Development*. London: Routledge.

———. (2002). *Transport Planning*. New York: Taylor and Francis.

Barwell, Ian (2011). *International Labour Office: Rural Transport in Developing Countries.* London: Intermediate Technology Publications.

Beck, Arne (2012). *Competition for Public Transport Services: Institutional Framework and Empirical Evidence of Bus Services in Germany.* New York: Springer.

Black, John (1981). *Urban Transport Planning: Theory and Practice.* London: Taylor and Francis.

Blow, Christopher (2012). *Transport Terminals and Modal Interchanges.* Oxford: Architectural Press.

Bonsall, Peter W., M. Quasim Dalvi and Peter J. Hills (2011). *Urban Transportation Planning: Current Themes and Future Prospects.* University of Leeds, Institute for Transport Studies and Abacus Press.

Chander, Jag Parvesh (1992). *Delhi is Doomed without Metro.* Delhi: Central News Agency.

Christie, Angela, Dan Smith and Kate Conroy (2013). "Transport Governance Indicators for Sub-Saharan Africa"", *Working Paper* No. 95. Sub-Saharan Africa Transport Policy Program. IBRD/The World Bank

Cole, Stuart (2005). *Applied Transport Economics: Policy, Management and Decision Making.* London: Kogan Page Publishers.

Coyle, John J., Robert A. Novack, Brian Gibson and Bardi (2010). *Transportation: A Supply Chain Perspective*. Canada: Cengage Learning.

Date, Vidyadhar (2010). Traffic in the Era of Climate Change: Walking, Cycling, Public Transport Need Priority, Delhi: Kalpaz Publications.

Deshmukh, Pratibha (2010). *Urban Transport Planning and Management*. New Delhi.

Francisco, Stella Amor J. and Jayant Kumar Routray (2007). *Road Transport and Rural Development: A Case Study in the Philippines.* Bangkok: Asian Institute of Technology, Division of Human Settlements Development.

Gandhi, P., Jegadish (1998). *State Transport Undertakings: Structure, Growth and Performance*. New Delhi.

Gautam, Parashuram Singh (1992). *Transport Geography of India: A Study of Chambal Division, M.P.* New Delhi: Mittal Publications.

Gautama, Q.L. (2012). *Indian Railways a Journey*. Delhi: B.R. Publishing Corporation.

Glass, David (2012). *Freight Forwarding and Multi Modal Transport Contracts*. Routledge.

Golinska, Paulina and Marcin Hajdul (eds.) (2012). *Sustainable Transport: New Trends and Business Practices*. New York: Springer.

Gubbins, Edmund J. (1996). *Managing Transport Operations*. Kogan Page.

Guha, Sabita (1991). *Economics of Rural Transport*. Delhi: Daya Publishing House.

Halder, Dilip (2008). *Studies in Urban Transport*. New Delhi: Bookwell.

———. (2006). *Urban Transport in India: Crisis and Cure*. New Delhi: Bookwell.

Haq, Gary (1997). *Towards Sustainable Transport Planning: A Comparison between Britain and the Netherlands*. Avebury.

Hariharan, K.V. (2002). *A Text Book on Container and Multimodal Transport Management*. Shroff Publishers & Distributors.

Hibbs, John (2000). *An Introduction to Transport Studies*. London: Kogan Page Publishers.

Hull, Angela (2010). *Transport Matters: Integrated Approaches to Planning City-Regions*. New York: Routledge.

Humphreys, Matthew (2012). *Sustainability in European Transport Policy*. New York: Routledge.

Jarboui, Sami, Pascal Forget and Younes Boujelbene (2012). *Public Road Transport Efficiency: A Literature Review via the Classification Scheme*. Springer.

Jonathan H., Grossman (2012). *Charles Dickens' Networks: Public Transport and the Novel*. New York: Oxford University Press.

Jourquin, Bart, Piet Rietveld and Kerstin Westin (2012). *Towards better Performing Transport Networks*. New York: Routledge, .

Kassens-Noor, Eva (2012). *Planning Olympic Legacies Transport: Dreams and Urban Realities*. New York: Routledge.

Konings, J.W. (2008). *The Future of Intermodal Freight Transport: Operations, Design and Policy*. Cheltenham: Edward Elgar Publishing.

Kulshrestha, Daksh Kumar (1993). *Transport Management in India: In Special Reference to Bus Stations*. New Delhi: Mittal Publications.

Kumar, Navin and Nidhu Kumari (2012). *Conceptual Architectural Design of Indian Railway Intelligent Transportation Systems*. Springer.

Kumar, Sudhir and Shagun Mehrotra (2010). *Bankruptcy to Billions: How the Indian Railways Transformed*. Oxford University Press.

Leggate, Heather, James McConville and Alfonso Morvillo (eds.) (2004). *International Maritime Transport: Perspectives*. New York: Routledge, .

Low, Nicholas (ed.) (2012). *Transforming Urban Transport: The Ethics, Politics and Practices of Sustainable Mobility*. Routledge.

Lowe, David (2012). *Lowe's Transport Manager's and Operator's Handbook 2013*. London: Kogan Page Publishers, .

Maeda, Tatsuo, Pierre-Etienne Gautier, Carl E. Hanson, Brian Hemsworth, James Tuman Nelson, Burkhard Schulte-Werning, David Thompson, Paul de Vos (eds.) (2012). *Noise and Vibration Mitigation for Rail Transportation Systems*. Springer.

Mallard, Graham and Stephen Glaister (2008). *Transport Economics: Theory, Application and Policy.* Palgrave Macmillan.

Mees, Paul (2012). *Transport for Suburbia: Beyond the Automobile Age*. New York: Routledge.

Nilsson, Måns, Karl Hillman, Annika Rickne and Thomas Magnusson (eds.) (2012). *Paving the Road to Sustainable Transport: Governance and Innovation in Low-carbon Vehicles.* Routledge.

Oliver, Inderwildi and Sir David King (eds.) (2012). *Energy, Transport and the Environment: Addressing the Sustainable Mobility Paradigm*. Oxford University: Springer.

Pandey, N.P. (1990). *Geography of Transportation: A Case Study of Western Madhya Pradesh*. New Delhi: Inter-India Publications.

Perl, Anthony and Richard Gilbert (2009). *Transport Revolutions: Moving People and Freight without Oil.* London: Earthscan.

R. Black, William (2010). *Sustainable Transportation: Problems and Solutions*. Routledge.

Ramachandran, M. (2011). *Metro Rail Projects in India: A Study in Project Planning*. Oxford University Press.

Rao, Desari Panduranga (ed.) (1986). *Problems of Urban Transport in India.* Proceedings of the International Seminar held on April 20-22, 1985. Delhi: Inter-India Publications.

———. (1989). *Dimensions of Rural Transportation.* Proceedings of the International Seminar held on September 10-12, 1988. New Delhi: Inter-India Publications.

Rietveld, Piet and Roger R. Stough (eds.) (2012). *Barriers to Sustainable Transport: Institutions, Regulation and Sustainability*. New York: Routledge.

Rodrigue, Jean-Paul (2013). *The Geography of Transport Systems*. Third Edition. New York: Routledge.

Rothengatter, Werner, Yoshitsugu Hayashi and Wolfgang Schade (eds.) (2011). *Transport Moving to Climate Intelligence: New Chances for Controlling Climate Impacts of Transport after the Economic Crisis*. New York: Springer.

Savage, Christopher and T.C. Barker (2012). *Economic History of Transport in Britain*. New York: Routledge.

Schade, Jens and Bernhard Schlag (eds.) (2003). *Acceptability of Transport Pricing Strategies*. Elsevier.

Schramm, Hans-Joachim (2012). *Freight Forwarder"s Intermediary Role in Multimodal Transport Chains: A Social Network Approach*. New York: Springer.

Seiler, Thorben (2012). *Operative Transportation Planning: Solutions in Consumer Goods Supply Chains*. New York: Springer.

Sharma, Sanjay Prakash (2010). *The Geography of Transport Systems*. Delhi.

Simpson, Margaret (2004). *On the Move: A History of Transport in Australia*. Powerhouse Publishing.

Singh, Jagdish (1964). *Transport Geography of South Bihar.* Varanasi: Banaras Hindu University.

Singh, Mohan (2011). *Transport Geography*. Jaipur: ABD Publishers.

Sinha, P.C. (2002). *Tourism: Transport and Travel Management*. New Delhi.

Tiffin, John and C.C. Kissling (2007). *Transport Communications: Understanding Global Networks Enabling Transport Services*. London: Kogan Page Publishers.

Vaidya, B.C. (ed.) (2003). *Geography of Transport Development in India*. New Delhi: Concept Publishing Company.

Vasconcellos, Eduardo Alcantara (2001). *Urban Transport, Environment and Equity: The Case for Developing Countries*. Earthscan Publications.

Verhoef, E.T., M. Bliemer, L. Steg and B. Van Wee (2008). *Pricing in Road Transport: A Multi-Disciplinary Perspective*. Edward Elgar Publishing.

Waqif, Arif A. (2000). *Cooperative Development of Transport and Communications Sectors in South Asia.*

Wear, Andrew (2009). *Improving Local Transport and Accessibility in Rural Areas through Partnerships.* OECD LEED Forum on Partnerships and Local Governance Handbook No. 1. OECD.

Zusman, Eric, Ancha Srinivasan and Shobhaker Dhakal (eds.) (2011). *Low Carbon Transport in Asia: Strategies for Optimizing Co-benefits*. New York: Routledge.